# Stained Glass

## ADVANCED TECHNIQUES AND PROJECTS

# Anita & Seymour Isenberg

# Stained Glass

## ADVANCED TECHNIQUES AND PROJECTS

Chilton Book Company

Radnor, Pennsylvania

Copyright © 1976 by Anita and Seymour Isenberg
All Rights Reserved
Published in Radnor, Pa., by Chilton Book Company and
simultaneously in Don Mills, Ontario, Canada
by Nelson Canada Limited
Manufactured in the United States of America

*Library of Congress
Cataloging in Publication
Data*    Isenberg, Anita.
    Stained glass, advanced techniques and projects.
    (Chilton's creative crafts series)
    Bibliography: p.255
    Includes index.
    1. Glass painting and staining—Technique.
  I. Isenberg, Seymour, joint author.  II. Title.
TT298.I835    748.5'028    75-31848
ISBN 0-8019-6194-7
ISBN 0-8019-6195-5 pbk.

67890    4321

*To* Mother *and* Jimmy—
*Four Helping Hands*

# Preface

We use the word "advanced" to indicate exercises for those who, grounded in the basic techniques of this craft, look forward to a stretch of the imagination. In that sense this volume is a continuation of our *How to Work in Stained Glass* which endeavored to provide such basic information. We have avoided going over material covered in this earlier book, though we have of necessity reiterated some of it where the juxtaposition of new accomplishments involved elaboration of the old.

At the same time, the word "advanced" is elastic and we understand what may be progressive for one will be old hat for another. So that the novice as well as the seasoned worker may find much to enjoy, we have provided a wide measure of variation. Simple and difficult techniques are demonstrated and the projects become more complex as they progress, concluding with a challenge to anyone's capabilities as well as a unique utilization of the materials of the craft.

For purposes of clarity, we have divided projects from techniques, though many of the techniques are really projects and a good deal of the projects are multiple techniques! It pays to give as much form as possible to a teaching process and that is what this book is meant to be. There is no project or technique here that does not involve itself with points of reference for further productivity of the reader, whether in concrete sale of items or the sheer joy of working with stained glass.

We would like to thank the studios and craftsmen who contributed their projects and techniques to these pages. All objects not otherwise credited are the work of the authors.

# Contents

# Part 1
# Techniques

Contents

**Contents**

## Part 2
## Projects

# Part 3
# Appendix

# List of Illustrations

xviii

# List of
# Color
# Illustrations

# Part 1

# TECHNIQUES

*"The wrong way always seems
the more reasonable."*
George Moore

# Chapter 1

# SOME
# HANDY TOOLS

The standard tools used in the stained glass craft have been described by us in our earlier book, *How to Work in Stained Glass*. However, since that book was written, new tools have come into use; and we also need to discuss those tools relating specifically to the projects and techniques in this book. There are many devices we cannot even touch on; inventions crop up constantly.

It is a measure of the appeal of stained glass that so many ingenious aids and provisions have come upon the scene in recent years. Nothing, however, can take the place of your two hands; it is for their pleasure and exercise that we offer the endeavors herein.

## WIRE BENDING JIG

The purchase of this tool will be one of the smartest dollars you'll ever spend. The wire bending jig, while not specifically for stained glass, is one of those devices that will make you wonder how you've done without it all this time. Directions for its use plus appropriate bend patterns come with it (see Fig. 1-1); and if you are doing any sort of mass production wire work, it will save not only time but your fingers.

When Figure 1-1 was taken, we were in the midst of making fifty stained glass roses for a party; in order to save glass cutting, we decided to indicate the center with a fairly complicated wire bend. We did the first three or four by hand; then began to stick wires in our hair! We tried several different jigs, finally settling for the Archer shown in the picture. In the upper left, you can see just a few of the multitudinous bends we made with this jig, and below the rest of the portions of the rose. It is difficult enough cutting all this glass without having to fight the wire as well.

Fig. 1-1 Wire bending jig shown as it comes. Bent wires at upper left give an idea of its effectiveness. The center rose shows how these wires form the flower center.

With the jig, wire bending becomes simply a matter of setting the pegs in the proper holes and knocking out the shapes from a continuous strand of wire which is nipped away as each shape is formed. Doing your work "in jig time" is a phrase specially apt for this little tool.

FOUR-IN-ONE TOOL

It cuts, bends, shapes and punches; that's the word on the Little Giant® (Fig. 1-2), made by Albert J. Tatu, Inc. We will be describing a number of projects that have to do with metal in one shape or another; this is the tool that helps put them into one shape or another. You can get accurate bends for your steel rods and reinforcing rods; you can shape copper and brass by shaving or clipping; you can punch holes in metal up to ¼" thick. We utilize this last procedure to give solid brass banding a "see through" effect so that the glass backing can show the way we want it to. In addition to its many uses, the Little Giant is unobtrusive on the work table. For the little space it takes up, it wields a lot of aid.

CLIPPERS

In the years we have been working with sheets of copper and other metals, we have tried a number of shears but we have never

4

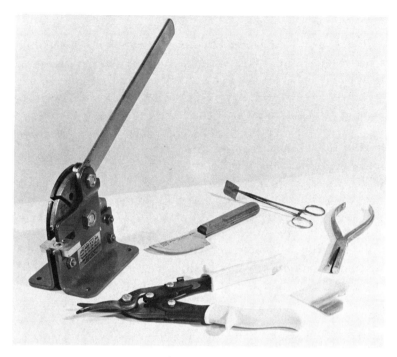

Fig. 1-2 A collection of tools: extreme left the Four-In-One tool. To the right in order: small lead knife (*Courtesy Glassmaster's Studio*), a forceps holding a piece of copper, French grozing pliers with an example of the type of inner curve they gnaw, and the Wiss Shears in the foreground.

come up with one that can match the Wiss M-3® clippers (see Fig. 1-2). This tool is all but universal; we have cut copper and sheet metal and brass and lead in lengths; we have sliced through soldered areas so thick even an iron would be able to melt only a little at a time and we have cut through steel nails—all with this tool. It is designed so as to give a comfortable grip and the greatest possible mechanical advantage for its size. When not in use (and it almost always is), there is a hinge lock to keep the blades closed.

SMALL LEAD KNIFE

For those who want a second or third lead knife and don't want to pay the price for another expensive imported one, here's a home-grown one, manufactured by Glass Masters, that is lovely (Fig. 1-2). And if you haven't got a lead knife at all, this is a good one to start with. It isn't complete with a leaded handle, but the blade is shaped just right and it cuts beautifully and provides the right impetus for getting loose ends of came placed just so. If you want a leaded handle, you can cut a notch in the wood and melt lead into it; the procedure isn't difficult. The cost of this item is approximately half of the professional leading knife. We use both; though we rely on our old imported standby, we have found this new little brother easy for students to use and habit-formingly easy to reach for ourselves.

5

## FORCEPS

If you have a friend who is a surgeon ask him about acquiring some old hemostats. This instrument is a type of forceps or self-holding clamp which can prove essential in dimensional stained glass work. We see this tool in the back of Figure 1-2, gripping a piece of copper in its jaws. The clamp is light, easy to handle and thin-nosed. The jaws are ridged so that when it grasps something it really holds on. The advantage of this is to permit you to reach into a sculptured object while holding whatever it is you want to solder gingerly but precisely by one handle. You needn't concentrate on holding the handles closed. Once the piece is soldered, the lock is opened by the merest pressure.

No routine hardware shop tool will offer this ease and stability. The closest you can get to it is a needle-nose pliers; and that's like using two thumbs to thread a needle. If you can't acquire this item when its days in the operating room are over, you can get one new from a surgical supply store. Ask for either a straight or curved (depending on your preference) Kelly® hemostat. If you want a slightly different variety that grips with small teeth directly from the front, ask to see an Allis® hemostat. Many physicians who are stained glass enthusiasts use such items to advantage; you can too.

## FRENCH GROZIERS

Figure 1-2 shows these groziers to the right with, under them, the piece of glass they have just been employed on. Note the small but technically perfect inner curve. This is shown more forcefully in Figure 1-3. These groziers are fairly new on the stained glass scene and very welcome. There is practically nothing else that does this particular job so precisely. However,

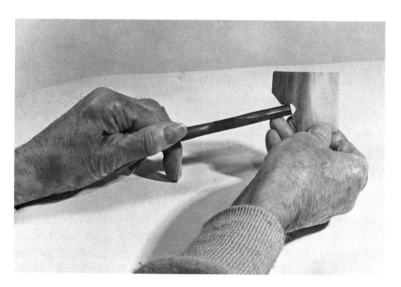

Fig. 1-3 The French grozing pliers at work.

Fig. 1-4 The plaster bowl and spatula. Under it is an old mold of Swedish steel into which the wax at the bottom left hand of the picture may be melted. In the background is an aluminum printing plate, cut to a shape on the right.

unlike most other stained glass tools, that is all they do. So if you do not intend to cut such shapes, don't buy them.

These groziers are composed of two rounded, teethed jaws which make wonderful nibblers. You can channel almost all the way through a piece of glass this way and achieve astounding key-in-lock patterns (see Chap. 2), whereas the ordinary grozing pliers, with its square jaws, would long since have snapped the glass. Keep this in mind as you gradually supply your workbench.

RUBBER BOWL AND SPATULA

When we discuss mixing plaster for molds, this is what we do the mixing in (Fig. 1-4). You can use a coffee can, plastic wastebasket or what have you, but you'll have a lot easier time of it if you get one of these. Having enjoined your physician, now give your dentist a break. He can probably get one of these for you free from his supply house. While he's at it, let him get you some dental wax as well (shown below the bowl). We use this wax to make lead castings, a process described in *Stained Glass Lamps.*

*Aluminum Printing Plate*   On the back of Figure 1-4, we show an aluminum printing plate. Print shops throw lots of these away every day. The ink comes right off them with most ordinary solvents and you have a great source for metal patterns without having to go into copper or brass. You can't make metal forms from this material because it's too light and won't solder; but when you have any pattern you are going to be repeating, whether part of a larger design or a design of its own, you can save constantly re-working it in paper by cutting it out of one of these press plates with a special pattern scissors. The aluminum

7

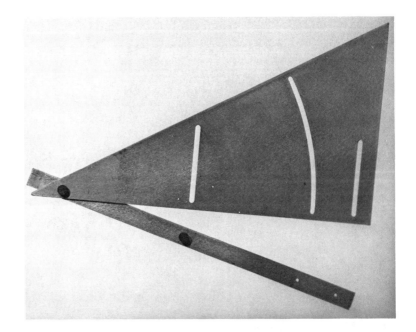

Fig. 1-5 The Timesaver. (*Courtesy Cookson and Thode*)

Fig. 1-6 The contour gauge taking a curve from a bent panel.

cuts as readily as paper. It tends to slide on the glass surface to a greater extent than paper, but you will soon learn the few tricks to controlling it. A reference file of metal patterns—inexpensive, permanent and accurate—can be built up rapidly.

THE TIMESAVER® JIG

All the items we have discussed are time savers but this one goes by the name as such (Fig. 1-5). Manufactured by Cookson and Thode, it's an ingenious device, adjustable to allow the worker to readily cut panels, strips and any irregular geometric shapes as well. When you need a quantity of accurately cut pieces—for lamps, window panels, candleholders—with a minimum of breakage, you might keep this jig in mind. It's simple but sensible.

CONTOUR GAUGE

You needn't let a three-dimensional object throw you a curve, you can take one directly from the surface of this gauge (Fig. 1-6). Then you can duplicate it elsewhere as a form in metal from which to make a mold to make more of the original.

Figure 1-6 shows this gadget in use. It consists of two metal rods which sprout a series of stiff copper wires riding free within the metal. Pressure against a contour pushes the wires inward, leaving a negative impression among the ones that remain, thus giving an exact duplicate of the form you either wish to measure or transfer. Since the tool is flat, you may lay it on a piece of pat-

Fig. 1-7 A new foiling device made by Lamps Ltd. (*Courtesy of Lamps Ltd.*)

9

tern paper and, using a sharp pointed pencil, guide it along the wire curves. When you're done, a tap on the wires from the other side will level them and you are ready for the next encounter. We find this tool especially useful in transferring the curves of either bent panel lamps or small pieced Tiffanies for which we want to make molds. The Contour Gauge® is sold in most hardware stores.

FOILING DEVICE

A new device by Lamps Ltd. has been made for foiling small pieces of glass (Fig. 1-7). The copper foil is placed on the back wheel and the tape comes off onto the front roller as the backing is stripped off by the middle chisel-edged metal section. The curvature of the front wheel bends the tape neatly over the edges of the glass as the operator turns the glass. Quick and easy foiling is accomplished with this device. It's a real boon to anyone making small pieced Tiffany lamps.

# Chapter 2

# DESIGN TECHNIQUES

Designing for stained glass can be as simple as one, two, three . . . four, five. Roman numerals, as you can see in Figure 2-1, make first rate designs. So do Arabic or Chinese characters. So does our good alphabet.

You don't have to know how to draw to be effective in stained glass designing, but you must learn to think in terms of background and foreground and in terms of how break lines must run and, more important, how they must not run. You must recognize the power of geometric shapes and how they may best be used. The most powerful window of this nature that we have seen is shown in Figure 2-2. Let's look at it more closely.

## THE POTENT TRIANGLE

At first glance, there are triangles all over the place; then, as the eye begins to absorb the initial thrust of the design, the foreground triangles inside their large circles stand aside a little and allow the background pattern to be seen. These triangles are really a second foreground; the true background is composed of the pieces between. But we are never allowed to get there, because by the time we have discovered this, the central figuration, which is the basic design, again takes over and fragments, right before our gaze, into interior patterns which reflect the outer shell. The eye is bounced back and forth like a beam of light; then the circular formation comes into play and leads us to another complex. In this fashion, the eye is never still but rather scoots over the surface missing some detail in one area, to be sure, but picking it up in another. Repetition is instinctive to this type of design. It is a beautiful example of a single spatial gesture defined and redefined through linear quality alone. With the addition of color (see color section), this logic of line takes on dimension as well.

Fig. 2-1 An interesting design using Roman numerals with break lines irregularly placed.

Fig. 2-2 The Mercedes Window of the Benzel-Busch Agency in Englewood, N.J. The repetitive design is the Mercedes symbol. The 8 feet high and 4 feet wide window was designed and fabricated by Lamb Studio. (See color section)

That is not to say all windows must look like this; but it demonstrates that designing for stained glass must take place within the particular harmonies of the linear quality chosen. What incites the purposeful motion of the eye upon this window is the play of light designed into it through line and color and arrangement; color choice is based on the line flow and cannot be made until this is finalized. This finalization is what design is all about.

LINES AND SPACES

As much creativity goes into what doesn't appear in a design as what does. What doesn't go in shows negatively as spaces between the lines that do appear—rather similar to the pauses in music or dramatic speech. This restrained aspect allows the statement greater power. So in starting a stained glass design, we will

Fig. 2-3   A beginning design sketch. (*Courtesy Lamb Studio*)

14

Fig. 2-4   Final drawn design.
(*Courtesy Lamb Studio*)

decide what we are not going to place as well as what we are. Let's look at a few designs.

Figure 2-3 shows a planning sketch for a religious window. This is a completely different pattern from Figure 2-2; not only for what is there but for what isn't there. The effect is not forceful but calm; there is no scurrying of the eye because no lines have been placed to stimulate motion. In fact, no background has been decided on but you can see that a lot of space is left over. Free space is generally calming; once you enclose space between lines, you can make it jump or you can let it flow, depending on how you place the lines within the space.

Against the quiet background wash of Figure 2-3, a complex foreground design is being drawn; a lot of space will be necessary to give it the proper emphasis. Figure 2-4 shows this type of de-

15

sign in completed form. Everything but this central portion has been left out; the surrounding space is a quiet grid of lines that serves only the purpose of complete subservience to the central quality. The problem with complete subservience, however, is that its boring—which in itself is a quality that may be distracting. We want boredom out of the picture! So flints, those small corner triangles which will be colored glass pieces, are placed in this background grid to compensate for the even flow of almost clear glass between the grid lines. But even in placing the flints, one must be careful not to create a surge of movement that will distract from that all-important central area. So the flints are placed exactly evenly on both sides, balancing whatever small movement may occur and bringing the eye back where the designer wants it.

## DESIGNING AND DRAWING

Now compare the two windows in Figures 2-2 and 2-4 once again. Both have a graphic foreground and both a background; but the background of Figure 2-2 is in motion, emphasizing its foreground, while the background of Figure 2-4 is still, emphasizing *its* foreground. So what have we learned? We've learned that Figure 2-4 which is a drawing is subject to different rules than Figure 2-2 which is a design. That is not to say that one is a better window than the other from this standpoint alone, but that effects are achieved by taking into account what reverberation, if any, you allow between the elements of your conception; and this in turn depends on whether you have a drawing or a design.

Look at it this way. Repetition in the background of Figure 2-4's basic endeavor would only be confusing; a single pattern in one circle from Figure 2-2 against a bland grid would leave us flat. What has been placed in one window has been left out of another. The logic for this is basic to all good stained glass designing.

## THE GEOMETRIC PATTERN

*Repeating Line*

Lest you think we have (to coin a phrase) drawn the line too sharply between a design and a drawing, we will take another geometric example. Figure 2-5 shows such a window being planned. The basic foreground elements are in place as well as a small amount of background lines to see how they fit. The focal point of the window is up top at the lettered area. This has been emphasized in two ways: by curvature of lines (lines curve nowhere else in the pattern) and by radiating lines from the top semicircle which indicate a force beneath them.

Fig. 2-5    Design in preparation. (*Courtesy Lamb Studio*)

One other foreground element, a cross, is going into place since this is a religious window. This central cross will travel the length of the window and the eye is meant to alternate between this feature and the arch. At this point, it was undecided whether to emphasize the cross even further by giving it very dark glass as shown in the bottom of the sketch. At the same time, the cross figuration is being carried right through the background as lines parallel to the top horizontal bar cross the pillars of the arch. Overemphasis of the central cross would demean this repetitive pattern and the cross was not darkened in for the final design.

A question also arises as what to do with the squares formed by the background crosses. To leave them open would make the background crosses too harshly competitive with the foreground. Therefore, further religious geometrical designs are being fabricated to fill these spaces in. Now, in just this much window, a lot

Fig. 2-6 Completed design.
(*Courtesy Lamb Studio*)

has been provided for the eye to read. A basic statement has been conceived, instituted, repeated and fleshed out.

Figure 2-6 shows this type of window completed. You have no trouble making out the central arch and cross and the radiation of arches and crosses that flow into immeasurable distance beyond, even while your attention is caught by the central cross. The lettering further establishes the curve of the main arch. The designed background squares give a rich effect to the whole, while allowing the eye a rest from following the ripples of the foreground. This makes those ripples seem extensive. The eye is easily fooled by lines that complement or interrupt one another. The typical example is the old puzzle shown in Figure 2-7. Line A may look shorter than line B but it is the same length. The lines surrounding it fool the eye. Any linear design takes this effect under advisement. But a design that employs actual figuration cannot do this. The eye would be confused by the introduction of repetitive figures as background design.

18

A                                                B

Fig. 2-7   An optical illusion.

*Little Background*

One of the simplest and most conclusive geometric designs is the circle or "bull's eye." Figure 2-8 shows such a design within a window. Here the background is compressed; it's formed directly by the foreground circles between the areas they meet. In fact it is sometimes debatable which is background when clear rondels are used and colored glass make up the spaces between. The bordering design is dissimilar on two sides; this is a choice for the designer when contemplating this type of window. Don't fool yourself into relegating this pattern to a simple process; there's a lot of cutting and fitting to be done here.

We have known workers to contract for this type of window and assume that because the rondels don't require cutting, a quick job can be done; no such luck. A window shouldn't be designed simply for haste of preparation anyway, but if haste is

Fig. 2-8   Typical rondel window pattern.

19

what you want, don't assume this design will provide it. This is a strict geometric repetitive rhythm; any discrepancy in the elements will be instantly noted by the eye because of the tremendous compactness that goes with the pattern.

*Extensive Background*

Contrasting widely with the above is Figure 2-9. Here we see a wide background of rectangles of clear glass which give us plenty of space to contemplate the ranging border. This panel demonstrates that a foreground need not be in the center. Here the foreground is in the upper portion because of the placement of this particular window; from the standpoint of design alone, it could have come from the bottom as well—or even from one side. Off-center foregrounds can be most effective. Toward the center of the window we see a further development of the basic geometric pattern into a convoluted section of design. This

20

breaks up three (note the odd number) of the background panels into an extensive background on their own, giving the window the effect of a panel within a panel. This effect is enhanced by the winding path of the vine and flowers against the strict geometric march of the border above. This double foreground, if you will, is tied together by a direct flow from the central point of the border as a spread downward. It is really very clever. The obvious choice of design would have been to duplicate the border from below. This would crowd the background, narrow the window and give a smothered feeling. Yet, with just the upper border design, the window would look unfinished. That central figuration with its tiny pattern ties the upper and lower sections of the window together and gives a further feeling of space to the design by adding to the impression of an extensive background display. If it were only the slightest amount larger, it would conflict with the lines above; as it appears, it's in perfect harmony.

## THE FIGURED PATTERN

A figured pattern need not imply an actual drawing. Figure 2-10 shows a central figured element and a noncompetitive background of straight lines which suspend the central core in magnificent solitude. Only when the background is far enough away from the center so no intrusion on the design is possible is some further ornamentation introduced in the shape of a filigreed border. And this is done very quietly and is instantly modified by an actual border of standard rectangles. There is a lot of space left around the center so the eye remains fixed in that area. Imagine that central pattern carried throughout the background. The whole thing would shout at you in a tangle of conflicting lines; it's the difference between noise and music.

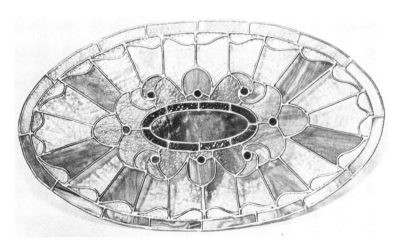

Fig. 2-10 Oval window demonstrating central figuration against a geometrical background. (*Courtesy Anita Isenberg*)

21

THE DRAWN PATTERN

*Little Background*

When a central design is an actual drawing, it can be emphasized by two methods: leaving a lot of background space or
leaving very little. In Figure 2-11, we show a drawing which
leaves very little background. The ship takes up almost the entire
panel. The space below is all ocean, what space is left above
between the sails is all sky. The ship is not only central to the
panel, it is the panel.

Consider it another way: with plenty of open space left around
it. The emphasis would now be balanced between the ship and
the sea and the sky—a different conception but still valid. However, if only slightly more space were given than is shown, we

Fig. 2-11 Design for a ship
panel. (*Courtesy Lamb Studio*)

22

Fig. 2-12 The preceding design cut to pattern. (*Courtesy Lamb Studio*)

would have a designing problem. There would not be enough space alone to balance the ship so we would have to start adding clouds or seagulls to it; and each such designed element would start to draw the eye from that central ship design.

Here the background was compressed as much as possible so that it could all be unobtrusively brought into the picture. Now there is no distraction from the foreground; what background there is actually reaches into the foreground to provide motion—similar to the technique used in Figure 2-2.

Figure 2-12 gives some idea how, once it's formulated and fleshed out, the sketch is re-skeletonized for the cartoon from which it must be cut. No sketch, regardless how cleverly it is designed, will work if it cannot be cut out of glass. It may seem an extraneous reminder but it is all too often overlooked in the sat-

23

isfaction of acquiring a balanced, perfect design. After all, you don't want to end up having to make a watercolor out of it.

*Extensive Background*

Figure 2-13 shows a central pattern which, to all intents, has no background whatever. Actually, its background is clear glass with squares so large that they emphasize the foreground. It is important to realize that this figure is all cut surfaces; obviously the linear quality is complex enough without obfuscating it with complementary or disparate lines anywhere in range. Yet the long, straight cross lines that are shown serve the purpose of support without getting in the way. They are almost bordering lines to the vase and so form a picture-frame effect—the four-square appearance of which is cleverly destroyed by the spread of the design over them.

This quality of a spatial arrangement reaching beyond its confines adds to the far-flung background perspective and emphasizes those foreground elements which the eye instantly seizes upon. The effect would not have been the same if the background squares were smaller; too many lines would be running

Fig. 2-13   Main window design. (*Courtesy Susie Creamcheese, Las Vegas, Nevada*)

back and forth. The effect might have been more striking if no background lines at all were present but this is architecturally impossible. Here the elements of the design serve to fill space with logic, courteously dependent on one another. Any repeating pattern, small though it is, is carried out some distance from the central figuration; most notably in the lower left panel.

THE THREE-DIMENSIONAL MOCK-UP

There may come a time when you will wonder what type of design to create for a particular room. This may be critical if you are doing a window for someone other than yourself; in many cases, a client will leave the designing entirely up to you. You don't want to put yourself in a position of pure guesswork, so you'll visit the room, plan a design and present it to your client. After the initial encounter, you'll probably forget what the room looks like and your client won't recall the design. When you're finished, you may have something that makes no one happy. One way to avoid this and strengthen your final conception is to make a mock-up of the room with the designed piece in place. It need not be as extensive as the one in Figure 2-14; but if the commission is a large one, it will be well worth the effort involved to show the client you have done your professional best to design a piece to suit his needs.

Take a camera with you when you visit the room and take plenty of pictures (see Glossary for photographing stained glass). Then cut out cardboard furniture and other room furnishings and put them in place if these items are to play against the projected design. Now draw your pattern and see what it does to this three-dimensional room. It should do something. If it has no effect at all, you had better modify or re-plan it. Perhaps it has too much effect; from a practical aspect it might overpower the room. It might cut the light from necessary areas or overilluminate others. When you have decided, meet with your customer so that he agrees with what you plan to do. Mock-ups

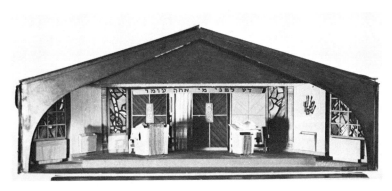

Fig. 2-14 Three-dimensional mock-up of projected windows. (*Courtesy Lamb Studio*)

25

Fig. 2-15 An "impossible" cut done well. The pieces of glass fit exactly.

usually impress clients; they see you have been working and they are able to visualize, probably for the first time, what their stained glass will be like to live with. The average mock-up takes about an hour; it is well worth it in terms of understanding the interplay of parts—which involves in larger aspect the art of exploiting all the elements in a given room toward a statement of some purpose.

DESIGNING VERSUS CUTTING

In professional studios, the designer and the craftsman are not always the same person. This can lead to areas of noncommunication where impossible cuts are inadvertently placed into the design. Usually these are ruled out in the normal course of events. Among hobbyists, though the designer and craftsman may be one person, you may wear different hats for each and present yourself with impossible cuts. In fact as the designer, you may resent feeling such cuts are impossible; occasionally you may be right.

As shown in Figure 2-15, sometimes cuts, purposely designed

26

to show the skill of the cutter, will enhance a fairly standard pattern. While it is true that only another glass person will see and applaud such posturings, it's fun to think that somewhere, maybe, someone will see and appreciate this tricky design formation. A lot of this depends on how good a designer you are and how effective a glass cutter. But then, you'll never really find out unless you try. Like any other designing trick, however, this one is most effective when used sparingly.

# 3 Chapter

# SURFACE TECHNIQUES

FLAT SURFACES

The following processes involve utilization of glass surfaces for entwining, engraving or embedding. They can be used separately or mixed within the same project. Each method provides another way to go which, when used wisely, gives a further sophistication to the worker's portfolio of designs.

*Fusing*

*Glass to Glass*    In its simplest form use window glass and glass stain; try this before going on to make fusings of stained glass. The fish in Figure 3-1 is a good example of fusing at its least complex. The shape was first cut out of ordinary glass in two pieces: the body and the tail. Multiple chips of glass colored with commercial stains were placed over the two original elements and two larger chips were placed at the apex of the front triangle. The fish was placed in the kiln and the temperature turned to 1400°F. This takes about one hour. At that heat we took a look; the complex was glowing a dull red. We turned off the kiln and allowed it to cool overnight—it is disasterous to expose a fused glass item to the air·after firing until it is stone cold. The picture here shows the result. A piece of nichrome wire serves to hang the object; if you wish to do this, the wire must be placed in the kiln under the glass prior to firing. During the fusing process, it will be embedded into the glass surface.

Another interesting example of a simple fused object can be seen in Figure 3-2. Again window glass was used and glass stain for the small pieces. The glass circle was cut and the parts arranged as you see them. A small brass finding was clipped onto the top surface. Then the glass was subjected to fusing temperature and you see the result.

28

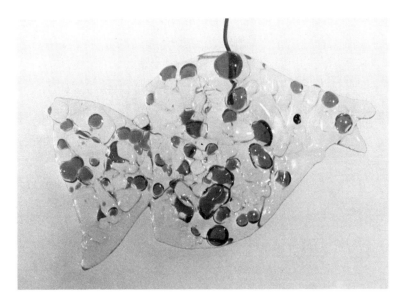

Fig. 3-1 An example of fusing window glass with "stained" pieces of glass.

Now let us go into something a little more complex using the same technique. In Figure 3-3 we show mushroom shapes cut out of window glass. The cuts are simple; the glass blanks will tend to look a little stubby at first. This tendency disappears as you apply the paint lines as shown. Any black firing paint will do. If the

Fig. 3-2 Shards of window glass stained and fused to underlying glass to make an attractive design. (*Courtesy Kay Kish*)

29

Fig. 3-3 Window glass cut to pattern (the pattern is at the left side of the picture) and trace painted for detail.

little painted circles tend to close up with the brush, wait until the paint dries and use a pointed stick to scrape the center open.

Using the design shown in Figure 3-4, cut a glass circle to fit the elements. You can fire the pieces first to preserve the trace lines and then paint the color in and re-fire or you can paint the color in very carefully now and only fire once. We like to save as much time as possible and try for the single firing.

Figure 3-5 gives an idea what these pieces look like from the glass blanks to the fully painted elements and in Figure 3-6 you see a completed project. There are five pieces of glass: two for the

Fig. 3-4 The same placed on its glass background ready for the initial firing.

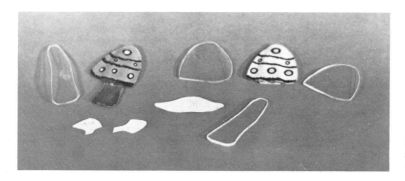

Fig. 3-5 Some individual
pieces shown from blank
stage to painted, fired and
rippled final stage.

large mushroom, one for each of the smaller ones and the background circle. This became two pieces on its own when it was
dropped, but don't despair if this happens. We glued the pieces
and got an interesting break line in the upper right portion. Only
one firing was necessary here; the trace paint and colored paint
maturation and the fusing of the pieces were accomplished simultaneously. Such little scenes with outspoken foregrounds are very
pleasant and you can make them en masse.

Where do you go from there? Figure 3-7 shows a fused piece by
Maurice Heaton, a modern master of the art. He doesn't make
them en masse.

Fig. 3-6 A completed fused
project made entirely of
window glass stained with
special paints. (*Courtesy Kay
Kish*)

31

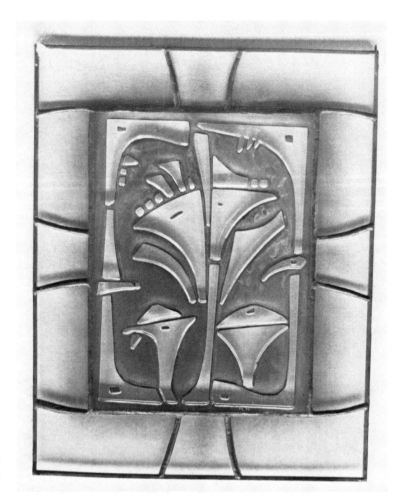

Fig. 3-7 Fused glass and stained glass combined by Maurice Heaton.

*Glass to Ceramic*   A variation of fusing glass to glass may work very well though difficulties abound. Figure 3-8 shows a ceramic hanging which contains fused glass in its center. The glass is red. When hung against a wall, it reflects light in a twinkle of ruby flashes; and against a window, the central core presents a steady outpouring of fire.

The problem with fusing glass to clay lies in the different coefficients of expansion of the two materials which makes for cooling fractures. This doesn't mean that fused glass and clay cannot work together. The clay is first prepared to receive the glass and is fired; the glass is then fused to its predetermined shape and the two elements can be glued together. It is preferable to accomplish an actual fusing; but unless you are a skilled ceramist, you may find a lot of frustration experimenting along these lines.

32

Fig. 3-8 Glass and ceramics. The fused glass is in the center of the clay backdrop.

*Stenciling*

*Templates to Glass*    Stencils for painting onto glass surfaces probably fill boxes and boxes in old stained glass studios. Such transfer templates are used whenever a design must be accomplished across multiple surfaces and whenever silk screening is not desirable. We see examples of such stencils in Figure 3-9. Notice the fine designs that can be made, providing the material used for the template is strong enough to maintain it. Stencils are cut out of tough paper (special stencil paper) or thin metal,

33

Fig. 3-9  Stencils and knives. The upper left stencil is paper; the rest are metal.

depending on how long you want them to last or how much work you expect to get out of them. Figure 3-9 shows a stencil cutting kit and to the left of it a stencil we have cut out of stencil paper. Even with limited use, we have lost a portion of this stencil; the top arm leading to the outer square has torn off. We knew these arms were the weakest portion; losing one of them, before the job was done, leaves only one alternative—cut a new stencil. Why not glue on a new arm? Because loss of the first one is a warning the whole piece is getting weak. Repairing a paper stencil is time consuming and to have it give out in another area after going through the labor of repairing the first is frustrating.

Below and to the right in Figure 3-9 are stencils cut out of metal. You can use thin copper or, our favorite, the aluminum printing plates described in Chapter 1. Obviously you cannot employ stencil knives on metal. When we make metal stencils, we use a flexible shaft tool, such as the Dremel® Moto-Tool, which is similar to a dentist's drill. Such tools can be equipped with all sorts of cutting wheels and edgers and if you want this type of permanent template you must use something like this to cut it. There are metal shops that will make stencils to your drawing if you don't want to invest in cutting them yourself. But there is no reason the ordinary craftsman would need a metal stencil; it is really a studio device. Many studios use them as master stencils from which to cut the paper ones. Your purposes will no doubt be satisfied with a paper stencil that will do, for a limited time, exactly the same job as the metal one.

34

*Using the Stencil   Accentuate the positive.* The glass blank is cut to exact size but before the stencil is applied, the entire surface of the glass is coated with paint and allowed to dry. Then the stencil is hand held and a dry paintbrush with strong bristles is used to scrape out the open spaces. Blow the dry paint away as you work, making certain you don't move the stencil over the paint. This background is tough enough not to flake off just from the pressure of the stencil alone. When you remove the stencil you should have an exact duplicate of the paper pattern.

*Don't eliminate the negative.* In this method, the stencil is positioned exactly over the glass blank and either held firmly by hand or taped into position so it will not move. The proper paint—usually a Stencil Black,® the same employed for silk screening—is used. With a substantial paintbrush, the paint is worked into the opened areas of the stencil, taking care that it does not flow beneath them. A thick consistency of paint is critical. Also critical is the flatness of the stencil against the glass. The thinner the stencil the better; the thicker it is, the more difficult it becomes to apply the paint throughout the design. Remember, the whole object in making a stencil is to speed up the work; if you have to fight the stencil, something is wrong. Once the surface is painted over, lift the stencil away and you should have its negative impression left behind on the glass (Fig. 3-10).

*Etching*

In order to properly etch glass, you need three materials: a proper etching surface, a proper etch and a "resist" material.

*The Etching Surface*   In order to be etched, glass must be "flashed." This is done in the factory by placing one color over another at the time the glass is made. Thus a blue color can be applied over white, clear, or yellow glass. Flashed glass can be

Fig. 3-10   Using the stencil. Paint is applied at the proper consistency so as to seep through the slots provided.

Fig.3-11 Items used for etching. The most dangerous is hydrofluoric acid in the plastic bottle in the background. The etching cream poses no real problem and is best to experiment with.

purchased at any store selling stained glass. The purpose of using flashed glass is to remove the top color to some imaginative or practical purpose, allowing the bottom color to show through.

*The Etching Material*    Figure 3-11 shows some of these. In the center is the most commonly used and the most efficient etching material, hydrofluoric acid. The acid is dangerous and should not be used without proper precautions. On the left is the milder Velvet® Etching Cream made by Rousse. This is slow working but for the beginning etcher might be worth trying for simple designs. It creates no noxious fumes as does the acid and will serve for small areas.

*The Resist Material*    The etching process must be carefully controlled since you want only certain areas of glass eaten away; the remainder should not be touched. The resist material is used to preserve the areas you don't want etched. It is first spread all over the glass; those portions you want etched are then scraped away.

Resist material comes in several forms; one is shown in Figure 3-11. The open jar contains an asphaltum mixture which is coated over the glass surface to be etched. Those portions where etching is required are scraped out of the medium either by etching sticks shown in the bottom of the photograph or, if finer lines are required, by the pen points seen to their left. Resist material can be obtained from Stewart-Clay Co. (see Sources of Supply).

For our purposes, we use acid and a resist material of clear Con-Tact® paper. The piece of glass to be etched is wrapped in Con-Tact paper pressed absolutely flat. The design portion of the glass is to be exposed to the acid and is cut out of the Con-Tact paper with a sharp knife. In Figure 3-12 we show the piece of glass after it has been through the acid bath still wrapped in its Con-Tact paper. Only the lettering has been affected; this portion of glass shows the bright yellow color below. In Figure 3-13, the entire project is shown with a red flashed glass. The rest of the details in this window are painted. Here you see an example of etched, painted and pure stained glass used together.

*The Sanded Surface*

Figure 3-14 shows another effect that can be obtained from a flat surface. Here the glass is *dalle-de-verre*, slab glass, but it could as readily have been flat glass. The pieces are held together with epoxy cement according to an underlying pattern and, while the epoxy is curing, a coarse sand is poured over the surface. The excess is shaken off once the epoxy has become hard and you have a textured, rugged surface design. These make great outdoor displays for garden or property line markers; a number of them, cemented together, can form a colorful fence either alone or intermixed with wooden sections. You can acquire an even more roughened surface by employing crushed glass instead of sand; or, if this makes the outline too raw, before epoxying the slab glass or flat glass together, run crushed glass over it and put the mixture through the kiln to fuse the two.

Fig. 3-12 Glass wrapped with Con-Tact paper. The design is cut out and glass is placed in bath with etching solution.

37

Fig. 3-13 The completed window center with etched, painted and stained glass. (*Courtesy Lamb Studio*)

Fig. 3-14 Rough sand technique with epoxy and slab glass.

Fig. 3-15 Mosaic. (*Courtesy Lamb Studio*)

## Mosaics

Glass mosaics can mimic tile and transmit as well as reflect light. If you have a lot of small pieces of scrap glass, you might attempt a mosaic; it is fun even though it takes forever to finish any sort of extensive project. In Figure 3-15 and Figure 3-16, we show two mosaics that could be done in glass. The smaller the pieces the more effective the work. The way to do this is trace out your design first. Then decide on the overall shape of the panel; cut a piece of plate or window glass, or acrylic sheet if you prefer, to this shape and you are ready to begin.

Attach your design under the plate glass and start filling in with pieces of glass bonded to the underlying plate glass with Duco® cement. We suggest this glue because it is convenient to use; it does not have to be mixed with a curing agent as does epoxy; it is strong and will not separate from the bond; it is inexpensive and dries clear.

In mosaic work, it is not necessary to use a glass cutter to produce the shapes you are after; wrap your scrap glass in a towel and give it a number of creative whacks with a hammer. The resulting small pieces should be approximated roughly in the areas of the design; when you are finished, the spaces between will be

39

Fig. 3-16 Another mosaic. An interesting way to use small pieces of glass. (*Courtesy Lamb Studio*)

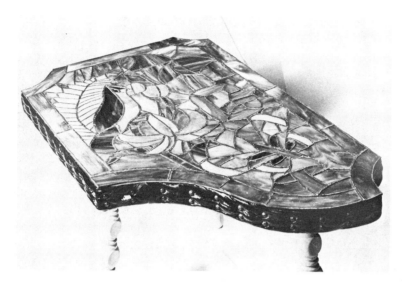

Fig. 3-17 Mosaic tabletop. Opalescent glass used throughout. (*Courtesy Larry Gargulio*)

filled with grout. The differential in light transmission between the dark labyrinth of grout and sparkling glass centers is highly dramatic (see Figure 3-17).

*Lamination*

Lamination is a cross over point between flat and dimensional surface techniques. Basically it involves some form of multiple glazing (see Glossary). The Farbigem technique, used so effectively by the Willet Studios of Philadelphia, is a form of lamination. The process involves plate glass, Plexiglas® and stained glass in a sort of bonded sandwich with the stained glass in the middle. Special adhesives are used to hold this mass together and spectacular architectural displays may be so created without the use of concrete or similar ponderous supporting matter. The Farbigem technique may also be used in small panels and free-form designs as well as sculptured items. The core of Plexiglas and plate glass is so strong that it will support many times its own weight of stained glass to either side, thus furnishing a sense of distance and foreground that is most effective.

Another form of glass in depth is *gemmaux*. This technique involves a layering of small pieces of glass glued or fused over one another; actually a mosaic in depth. Superimposition of colors presupposes a lot of skill; you can end up with disarray if they mix incorrectly. A bas-relief linear quality is inherent in gemmaux as in most multiple glazing procedures. Needless to say, if the layering effect is carried to extremes, you will need a pretty bright light source for your display to be effective. Here is our difference between lamination and multiple glazing. Multiple glazing does not superimpose colors. It attaches glass pieces in depth along their borders without covering one another. This

41

layering effect projects visual reach. Lamination involves covering one piece of glass with another; this changes the color. Many workers combine superimposition with multiple glazing, depending on what sort of result they have in mind—nothing wrong with that.

*The Melted Surface*

Very unusual effects can be accomplished by placing glass on a flat bed of kiln wash (see Glossary) and running the heat up to 1500°F or 1800°F. The glass will melt at those temperatures and start to run to greater or lesser degree; as the heat is turned off, the glass freezes in forms and patterns resembling multicolored inkblots. Take these whorls and runs of glass from the kiln, gently brush off the underlying wash and glue them onto other surfaces—either clear or colored glass—with Duco® cement.

This surface glass can itself be cut into patterns and placed within a larger design or it can, with its unique frontal display, be a design all on its own.

It is also possible to fuse into the underlying glass the previously melted portion to acquire inlays and overlays representing landscapes, firmaments, or maybe scenes from Shakespeare, depending on how your imagination fires. This type of undisciplined design formation cannot be calculated to any extent in advance; you may require three or four firings before you come up with anything worthwhile. Experiment with the temperature and look inside the kiln to see what type of shape is being formed and whether or not more heat is required. The more heat you apply, the more fragile your final result and the more difficult to separate it from the wash. But if one firing out of ten gets you a result you love, you will come out with a unique display on which you have spent very little labor.

DIMENSIONAL SURFACES

*Drapery Glass*

The multiple glazed surface is the first step in providing dimension. In the section dealing with lamination, we discussed this technique worked with small pieces of glass either superimposed or attached only along their borders. (See also Chap. 13, The Triple Glazed Bird.) However, a dimensional effect can also be acquired by using glass with a convulsed surface; this is the so-called drapery glass. This material is almost impossible to come by now; in prior years, it was factory made in great quantities to represent the flow of raiment in figures in religious pictorial windows. It is so textured that its presentation, even by itself, calls up association with clothing (Fig. 3-18). If you are lucky,

Fig. 3-18 Drapery glass cut for a window. (*Courtesy Lamb Studio*)

you might be able to buy a small piece of it, or maybe a sheet or two if you can find an old studio going out of business.

This glass is cut with some difficulty because of the multiple surface folds. In Figure 3-19, the glass is being fitted in place on the cartoon. The emphasis placed by this type of glass along its propulsive ridging makes the project stand forth. Drapery glass is often double glazed (see Glossary) to give it even more of a thrust outward. In Figure 3-20, we see the cut glass blank that will fit beneath the piece of drapery glass shown in Figure 3-18. Both

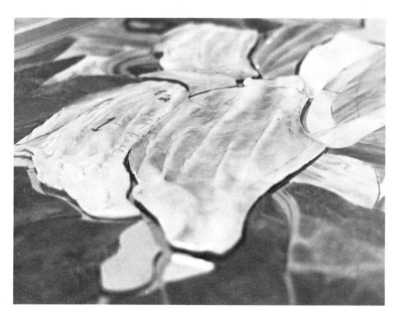

Fig. 3-19 Drapery glass being placed into the window elements. (*Courtesy Lamb Studio*)

43

Fig. 3-20 Glass blank used with the drapery glass cut in Figure 3-18.

pieces of glass will be held within an extra wide ¾″ lead came or each can be provided with its own lead and the rims of metal soldered together on the window.

*Sculpture*

Two or more surfaces held in different planes provide a more obvious spatial grasp than does one surface, no matter how cleverly designed. Free standing objects may be made in stained glass in two or three dimensions. In Figure 3-21, we see a Hopi Indian basically in two dimensions except for the overlay of his arms and the fact that some of his feathers slant forward.

In Figure 3-22, we see a bird that is completely sculptured. Glass plates comprise his head, body and tail; he is closed in on all sides. Surely this is a more effective display than if the bird were flat. This is a fairly obvious type of sculpture: a formed object.

The same design philosophy can apply to abstracts as well. Figure 3-23 demonstrates a new technique along these lines with a combination mobile and sculpture: the stained glass tapestry.

*Tapestry*

The stained glass tapestry technique features the use of hanging pieces of stained glass suspended on nylon-encased steel wire in long strands (see Fig. 3-23). These strands hang in series and on various planes to bring about a beautiful interplay of color. More color is always available to the eye dimensionally than in a flat surface. With a light colored wall which can be flooded with light as a back drop, the glass tapestry is very effective. Research is presently being done by Glassart of Arizona to utilize tapestry as a mobile. It would be an exciting object hung as a large mobile in an area with an abundance of light. But it doesn't have to be large. The beautiful tapestry shown in the picture is seventeen feet high by ten feet wide; you can make a smaller model, using heavy fishline as the background cables and the elements from which to hang your glass.

Fig. 3-21  Hopi Indian.
(*Courtesy Glassart Studio*)

45

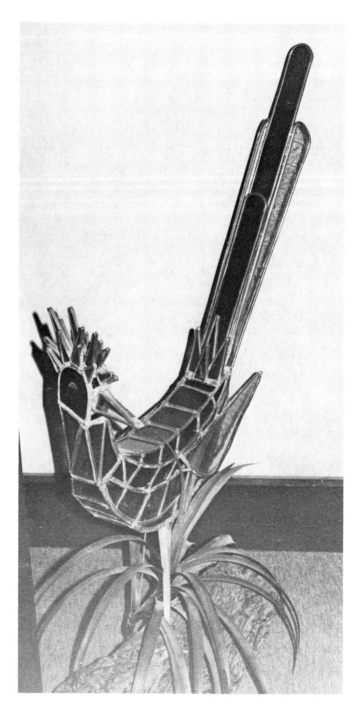

Fig. 3-22 Sculptured bird.
(*Courtesy Glassart Studio*)

*Lamp Panels*

The bent surfaces with which craftsmen are most familiar are lamp panels. If you don't want to get involved with bending your own glass yet, you can learn how to employ old bent broken panels to advantage. They contain a lot of admirable glass; all you have to do is recycle them to fit your requirements.

46

Fig. 3-23 Tapestry. Stained glass and nylon wire. (*Courtesy Glassart Studio*)

Figure 3-24 shows such a panel. It has broken in half and is useless—for a lamp, but not for such an item as a bent leaf which you might like to use in a display.

We have made such a pattern and you can see there is plenty of room for it on the broken panel (Fig. 3-24). We have already scored the panel for the first break. Bent glass is best

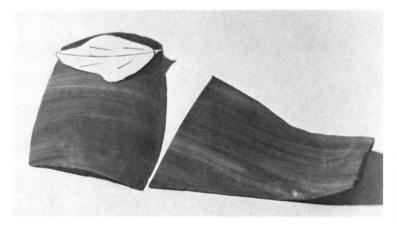

Fig. 3-24 A broken bent panel in process of being recycled into small bent objects. Here a leaf will be formed.

47

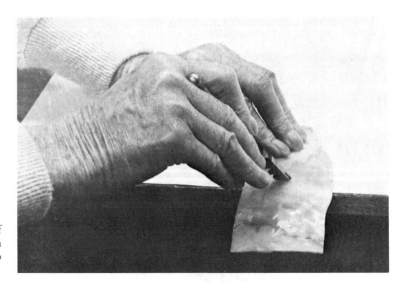

Fig. 3-25 Cutting a piece of bent glass. The pressure from the glasscutter is as close to the tabletop as possible.

scored by placing it in as much a position of rest as possible. Over a table edge is good (see Fig. 3-25); this takes the strain off the far edge and supports the area being scored. Once the score is made, the glass can be snapped along the table edge (see Fig. 3-26) or tapped from below. The same procedure is effected for each of the succeeding cuts with grozing pliers pulling off the small portions of waste. You are then left with a bent glass blank cut to size which need only be painted or simply placed and leaded to achieve a large, overall effect with little comparative effort. As for a supply of broken glass panels, studios and antique stores are usually glad to get rid of them.

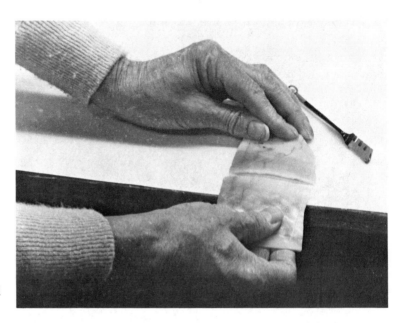

Fig. 3-26 The scored panel broken in two.

Fig. 3-27 The Bottle Ship.
(*Courtesy Marvin Riddle*)

*Bottles*

Another familiar bent surface is the bottle. There are a number of kits on the market to enable you to cut bottles, but you can accomplish this feat with just a glasscutter. Remove the bottle cap, hold the cutter on a surface level with the area you want to cut and turn the bottle against the cutter until it is scored on all sides. Hold it under very hot water and then very cold water and it will pop neatly apart.

For purposes of design, bottle bottoms fit in with a number of projects; they provide lovely rondels. This is mostly true of wine bottles, but unfortunately they are the hardest bottles to cut (beer bottles are the easiest, but they don't have desirable bottoms). The same process is applied except that a good bit of grozing will still be required to get the bottom into shape for a project. It is tricky work and dangerous as far as cutting yourself. Not only are bottles useful for their bottoms and the horizontal slices for either glasses or windchimes, but they can be utilized for vertical cuts. Figure 3-27 shows a sailing vessel made entirely of vertically cut pieces from several large wine bottles. The curves and bends are taken directly from the previous vessel to make this one. It's on sail.

# 4 Chapter

# PAINTING DETAIL AND TEXTURE

The idea behind impressing painted detail and texture on colored glass is to aesthetically amplify and complement the basic design. Improperly applied, such ornamentation diminishes an end result that may be dramatic enough on its own. Painted highlights, background or texture are meant to be unobtrusive; when they become the focus of the work, no matter how cunningly done or imaginatively conceived, the overall design suffers.

THE BRUSHES

In Figure 4-1, we show a number of brushes that may be used in glass painting. They are all expensive and you won't need them all unless you are going to be painting full time. The group on the lower left are tinting and mottling brushes; on the upper left you see stipplers and shaders. On the upper right is a Badger Blender® and the group on the lower right are scrollers and tracers. In addition you may buy square shaders and pointed shaders, long painters and short painters, cut liners and watercolor brushes, as well as grounding brushes, red sable brushes and ox-hair touch-up brushes. Since this is not a book on painting, we will indicate in this chapter only a few of the advanced techniques of this complicated art process.

GRINDING THE PAINT

Glass stainers paint is sold as a dry powder and *must* be mixed with whatever medium is called for (see Sources of Supply). Such a medium may be water, vinegar and gum agar (see Sources of Supply); it may be a nonspecific oil, or the paint may come with its own medium. Some fired paints are sold already ground and mixed with medium. In every event, the initial step where grinding is done is to make sure the powder is of an equal consis-

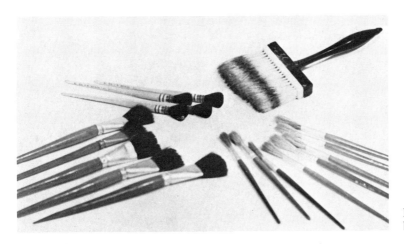

Fig. 4-1 A selection of
brushes for painting on glass.

tency prior to mixing. For this you need a pestle of heavy glass
and a grinding pallet (see Fig. 4-2). Once the paint is ground,
the medium is added (Fig. 4-3) to achieve the proper consistency—neither too thin to maintain a line with nor too thick to
flow—and the appropriate brush is then brought into action (see
*How to Work in Stained Glass*). In applying design lines, the action is straightforward with the use of a scroller or tracer. In
adding texture or modifying a designed background or emphasizing
or recessing the amount of light coming through the glass, many
methods may be used.

Fig. 4-2 Grinding the
paint.

51

Fig. 4-3 Taking the paint from the palette.

## ADDING TEXTURE

Texture is not altogether dependent on brushes. We have used feathers, fingerprints, palm prints, rubber stamps and heaven-knows-what to give novel textural effects; brushes are a standard safe bet all the same. In Figure 4-4, you see the original matt paint smear left by a tinting brush. Special paint called matt (see *How to Work in Stained Glass*) is generally used for its textural, background or shadowing qualities. Though this is by no means always the case, for the sake of clarity here, we use the term *matt paint* for soft texture and *trace paint* for hard detail.

We made the smear thin in consistency to show the bubbles that form their own pattern in this mixture. The addition of

Fig. 4-4 The original smear of paint we intend to texture.

more paint, mixed more strongly with a spatula, would provide a smear darker in color without the brush stroke lines and without the bubbles.

*The Toothbrush Effect*

Figure 4-5 shows what can be done with the smear shown in Figure 4-4 by passing a toothbrush over it. The smear must not be completely dry or it may flake away, nor should it be so wet that the bristles of any forthcoming brush become too saturated with paint to maintain their individuality. The texturing time varies with the consistency of the paint and you can only learn by experience. Notice the difference in the smear once the toothbrush has worked it over. The careless, "smeary" effect is gone and a sense of purpose has entered into it. Where to stop texturing depends on the worker. The toothbrush can be employed until only a hint of paint is left on the glass in even finer lines than are shown here, or the texture can be left as is. This must be decided before starting to texture so you can have some idea how fast you must work to accomplish your purpose before the paint dries.

*Shading*

Now imagine the same smear brought back again. This time we are going to try for a different result: wavy lines rather than straight, thin ones, such as we might find in a beard. For this we use a shader or a tinter and the strokes are wavy rather than straight across. In Figure 4-6, we can see the result of this process. To the left we have carried the waves further along than we have on the right and the paint here has become thin—though still indicative of the design we want to produce.

Fig. 4-5 Toothbrush texture.

53

Fig. 4-6 Wavy texture.

Both heavy and thin lines are sometimes essential within the same portion of glass. You must learn to control several factors of the stroke to accomplish this: wrist motion, degree of pressure on the brush, amount of sweep. The motion of your wrist can produce longer or shorter waves, thereby extending and thinning the paint line. The brush pressure affects the amount of paint that is swept off the glass and how much remains. The amount of your sweep with the brush depends on how much area you want each stroke to cover; the more area, the thinner the paint line; the shorter, the thicker.

Also you must take into account how often you clean your brush. Paint that the bristles pick up tends to dry rapidly. If you wipe this away immediately, you will maintain a fairly even brush figuration; if you do not, the painted bristles will tend to stick together and your brush figuration will blur. We don't like surprises so we clean our brushes after each stroke by wiping the bristles on a rag. Never clean them with any sort of liquid while attempting to make duplicative strokes. Theoretically it shouldn't make any difference, but impatience to continue the work may propel you to use the brush before it is dry; and you can ruin all the texture with one ill-advised stroke.

*Stippling*

Let's go back to our original smear. This time we let it dry longer than before since we don't intend to work *in* it so much as *on* it. This doesn't mean that you can let it dry completely by any means; but it shouldn't be "squishy." Now with your stippling brush come down on the smear with short jabs. As you do this, you will see the paint begin to thin in discrete areas; as you continue the stroke, these areas will widen with consequent diminishing of the paint.

Figure 4-7 shows this effect and, again, we have done considerably less stippling on the left than on the right. On the left, quite a lot of paint is left, giving a bumpy, almost ridged, surface. The right-hand portion shows what happens if the process is carried on; eventually as the paint dries and more and more of it is carried away with each stroke, you can practically see the circumference of the brush. You may want such circumferential detail to be stark or meld together; or you may prefer to stop long before this and maintain the marbelized impression of the thicker surface. You will notice the brush we have chosen to demonstrate with is a round one; we prefer this form for stippling though you can, of course, stipple with almost any brush as the inclination strikes you.

In Figure 4-8, you can see the stippling effect produced by stippling with a Badger Blender. The result is a much more even, yet grainier effect than that previously shown. The best brushes to stipple with are those that have wide surfaces; if you attempt to stipple with tinting or tracing brushes which come to an edge or a point on their surface, you will get only a smear.

*Blending*

In Figure 4-9, we present the original smear "blended" over the surface of the glass. The brush used is called a "blender" and the strokes are wide and smooth rather than short and jerky. A good blend stroke starts several inches before the smear and ends a good distance after it. In that way a natural flow is imparted to the paint. Strokes need not be, and in the main are not, limited direction-wise. As you can see from the strokes impressed on the

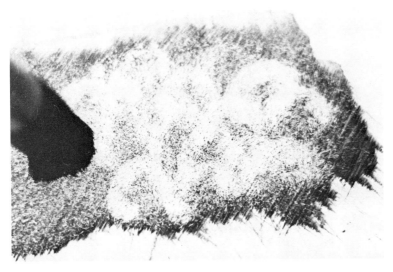

Fig. 4-7   Stippling.

Fig. 4-8 Stippling with a Badger Blender.

paint in the Figure 4-9, they go in several directions. The "blending" evens the paint with a specific smear so that it covers the surface. Again the longer the blending process is continued, the more paint is wiped away and the less remains. Because the blender's bristles are very soft, it takes a long time to remove a whole lot of paint. The blender's purpose is to spread paint.

*Stroke Combinations*

Some workers initially use the blender on all smears to obtain the maximum paint consistency before proceeding to textural modifications. Others rarely use the blender at all, preferring a harsh inconsistency of stroke.

Fig. 4-9 The blend.

Keep in mind that no painted detail is permanent just because the effect has been achieved in the "wet"; it may not fire the way you'd planned. Paint that is too thick may "layer out"—that is, it may dry in irregular thicknesses. This will only show up after the firing process. Paint that is too thin for the kiln, that will eventually burn away, may appear the perfect shading for the area in the unfired state. So while you should attempt to get your shading or texture as perfect as possible, it will take practice with the kiln as well as with the brushes, and inspiration, to discover what is practical and what is not. This applies only to paint that is to be fired; unfired paints cannot be manipulated in these ways.

It is fun to try different combinations of strokes and different thicknesses of paint. Keep a record of what you have done and the processes you have used so you will have an idea, after the glass has been fired, which work well and which should be modified or, indeed, discarded.

*Stick Lighting*

Figure 4-10 shows this process which can be defined as scraping away paint with a sharp pointed object to allow light through. It is negative painting, if you will, and can be used alongside paint lines as well as within large areas to trim, foreshorten or detail them with light. Special maple pencil sticks are sold for this purpose but you can use any pointed object that won't mar the glass, including manicure orange sticks. Even a sharp pencil will work, though it is not recommended since the point wears, leaving uneven lines in the paint.

Fig. 4-10  Stick lighting.

57

FIRING PROBLEMS

For those readers who have little experience in firing glass, we strongly suggest you read up on the procedure itself (see *How to Work in Stained Glass*) before attempting to understand the problems involved.

*Cloudy Glass*

If your glass turns cloudy, either you haven't cleaned your glass prior to painting or you haven't done so prior to firing. The best cleaner for glass, and the closest to hand, is the paint itself. Smear some on both sides of the piece of glass you are going to be working on and rub it around with a clean cloth until it is gone. It has a mild abrasive action and will pick up any debris on the surface. Your glass will come out polished and shining. When you are ready to fire, make sure the back surface of your glass is cleaned again. This will smudge as you are working; you'll probably be concentrating on the top side and may forget about the unpainted side.

Another fault leading to cloudy glass is a dirty kiln. What have you fired in it recently? Specks of carbonized material may

Fig. 4-11 Differences in fired and unfired paint. The dark, shiny surface of the left leaf shows a perfect firing. The right hand piece is as yet unfired.

be perched on the firebrick; as the hot air swells during the firing process, this material will rise and float about; as you cool the kiln, it may settle on the glass.

### Bent Glass

We bend glass purposely for certain projects, but for glass to bend on its own is disasterous. Unexpected bent glass can be due to firing on uneven surfaces of the kiln wash or even on a cracked or chipped firebrick or kiln shelf. A bent piece of glass foreshortens and will, of course, never fit within the pattern for which it was made. Bending of the glass surface will distort all painted lines as well.

If your glass does bend unintentionally during firing, it's better to start again rather than to attempt to flatten pieces of glass. Theoretically, if you place these on a flat surface and re-fire, they should flatten to size; in actuality, it rarely happens. Many times the glass cannot take the re-heating and unbending process; unless in very small pieces, they tend to crack. Color of the glass is another factor to keep in mind; many colors fade with refiring. And the time involved is rarely worth it. Keep all misbent pieces, however; you never know when they will come in handy.

### Shrunk Glass

Overfiring is the problem here. Glass tends initially to crawl together when it is overfired; as heat continues, it may soften as well. This plays hob with your pattern again, since the glass piece may be too small by as much as ⅛ inch all around and its painted surface will ripple and blur.

### Thin Paint Lines

Your paint lines may have looked fine during the painting cycle, but obviously they were not—since the kiln firing is the final judge. Probably the side to side consistency was uneven, allowing burnout along the width of a central thickness. Paint lines may be too thin in paint thickness as well as width. A black tracing line used to emphasize a detail should allow no light through at all. If yours does, then the paint was not thick enough or not mixed well enough to allow proper impregnation of the glass; burnout occurs this time from front to back of the line.

### Thick Paint Lines

This rarely happens due to firing. This is usually due to excessive applications or paint that was too thick to begin with. Paint lines can still end up appearing disproportionate if burnout of other lines has occurred around them. This occurs if part of the surface is painted but not fired the same day. Avoid "stale"

59

paint. Try to paint and fire the day's work at the same time so the consistency, weather and temperature remain constant for these areas. Trouble-free painting calls for the elimination of as many variables as possible.

*Frying of Paint*

This is the most common problem with firing paint. The cause is either overfiring or poor consistency of paint due to mixing, applying too much paint or layering paint by adding fresh paint to old. By "old" we mean paint that is already dry—whether one second dry or two days dry. If you have readied a piece of glass for firing and decide that one more line should be added to connect two dry ones, chances are the paint will fry at the point of attachment of the new line to the old ones. The heat makes it bubble up no matter how concise the layered surfaces may be. Some frying can be overlooked; most cannot. At its worst, frying leads to disruption of lines entirely; moderate frying may nibble chinks and holes along the surfaces of lines; mild frying may allow the surfaces to remain, but in a roughened condition rather than the smooth, shiny quality you should obtain. When the first two conditions prevail, you can do nothing but throw the glass away and repaint; with mild frying, you have a choice. You can leave it, especially if it isn't too extensive, and hope nobody will notice (except you: you will always know) or you can attempt to reheat the piece at a low temperature in hopes the roughened surface will smooth out. Do not add more paint; work with what is already there. Sometimes this technique works quite well. Never take the kiln all the way back up to the original temperature. Paint fires between 1100°F to 1200°F; when we try to improve fried lines we go to 1050°F or 1100°F. It depends on how the lines look at those temperatures; we peek through our top loader.

You can sometimes help this process by using certain spreading media which supposedly impel the fried paint to straighten up and fry right. Mineral oil is one we have tried, but we aren't too enthusiastic about these media. Fried lines tend to go their own way no matter what you use to coax them. Our feeling is that you can spend more time and energy attempting to re-cook fried lines than you would if you re-did the pieces from scratch having chalked (or painted) the matter up to experience.

*Sticking Glass*

Painted pieces may stick in the kiln—either to the shelf or to each other—much more readily than unpainted surfaces. If they stick to each other, you have placed them so they touch; with the heat, they will fuse together to that extent. If they stick to

60

the shelf, you probably have dribbled paint down one side or left some on the backside. There is nothing you can do in this instance except scrape the remains into the garbage and start over.

WAXING UP

When paint lines are to travel over several pieces of glass, it is essential that the craftsman knows how the totality will appear. It is also important that none of the pieces move during the process. To achieve both these ends, the glass is held firmly (either on a light table or on a window easel) with a material that is easily maneuverable, will grasp quickly and can be easily broken away with no harm to the glass. Beeswax is the classical material for this purpose. It is heated and mixed with resin for stiffness. The mixture varies with the season: more resin during the summer when the wax is runnier; less during cold weather when the wax is stiff. We use this wax for other purposes as well (see Chap. 14, The Menorah); it is handy to have around.

In Figure 4-12, we show how our wax is stored. To heat the wax, an old pot with tape wrapped around the handle to prevent burned fingers is fine; inside the pot we have soldered a metal bar to support our medicine droppers which we use to apply wax to the corners of the glass. These droppers will always get lost if not secured. When we are ready to use our wax for a project, we use a

Fig. 4-12 Pot-au-feu; if you like wax, that is. As long as you keep the dust out of it, you can continue to re-use it. The medicine dropper is also stored in the pot.

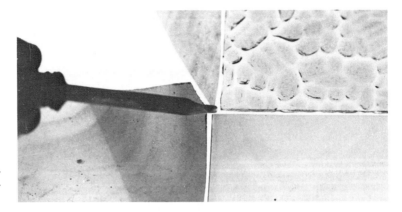

Fig. 4-13 Waxing up several pieces of glass preparatory to painting.

small burner (men, never cook your wax on the kitchen stove; divorce is inevitable) and stir the mixture as it melts. If you overheat the wax, a good bit of smoke will result; if you go beyond this, your wax may catch fire.

In Figure 4-13, we see several pieces of blank glass over which we want to place continuous trace lines. The medicine dropper is used to apply liquid wax to corners of the glass. Figure 4-14 shows the process of waxing completed with the glass standing immobile. The wax cannot get in the way of the paint which, in Figure 4-15, does its own thing over any surface it wishes to cover. Of course we have used a very simple design for demonstrative purposes; it would not ordinarily be essential to wax up for this amount of painting; the worker could hold and paint two pieces at a time. Figure 4-15 shows the design completed and the preparation for the glass to be broken away from the wax by the prying action of a spatula. Don't get careless here and try to use a thin object as a lever. The wax does grip firmly and unless you pry with a wide, flat surface you can crack a piece of glass or the light table surface. Figure 4-16 shows the pieces of disparate glass with continuous painted detail, ready for firing.

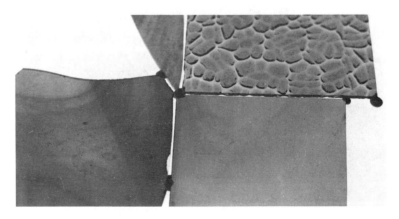

Fig. 4-14 The wax in place.

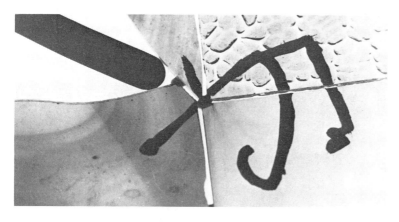

Fig. 4-15 The painting (such as it is) is completed and the glass is ready to be broken away from the wax.

## COMBINING TECHNIQUES

### The Painted Ship

Having discussed several painting processes, we now want to put a number of them together to show how they provide for the end result. We'll take our cue from Coleridge: "A painted ship upon a painted ocean." There are three panels in Figure 4-17; let's take them one at a time.

*The Ship in Lead*    This is the panel on the left. It represents a pictorial window using glass alone. The subject is a ship at sea and the three elements of the design are clearly apparent: the ship, the sea and the sky. As a leaded panel it is complete; as an artistic study it is lacking. No matter what our choice of line, no matter how brilliant the glass hues and tones, the conception cheats the eye. The mind's eye sees more than what is actually there. Skillfully executed, the end result is flat. Let us add some of this detail in paint and see what happens.

*The Ship in Detail*    The center panel is what the project would look like if it was disassembled and trace lines added. No tex-

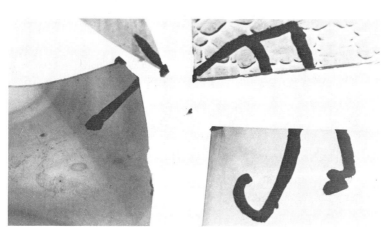

Fig. 4-16 The pieces of separate glass.

63

Fig. 4-17 The Painted Ship—shown in three stages. On the left, glass and lead. The center panel shows trace paint added. The right hand panel shows the completed ship. (*Courtesy Lamb Studio*) (See color section)

ture has been employed as yet, but look how the character of the entire picture has changed. Yet the detail added has not been so great as to override the basic design. Some rigging has been placed at the top to emphasize the ship's forward motion and at the bottom the waves have been filled in along with a school of dolphins; all this motion flows ahead, carrying the ship with it. Immediately, this much painting—all black trace paint, remember—has transformed the vessel from a motionless collection of lines to a purposeful, thrusting object.

To add to the sense of activity, detail has been added into the sails, giving an impression of the sails being filled with wind. Just the few lines and dashes shown are enough. Most of the concentrated painting has occurred on deck; the weight of this helps settle the vessel in the water. The right side of the hull is completely covered with paint; this will be textured with a brush or a stick light for a final presentation to represent wooden planks. Two of the background sails have a coating of "wash"—very thin trace paint applied with a tinting brush to highlight the foreground sails. Nothing has been done to the third component, the sky, because no trace lines are possible here other than to indicate a cloud formation. There is no room for a cloud nor any reason for one design-wise (see Chap. 2).

*The Ship in Passage*   In the right hand panel, the detailed and textured project makes weigh. Matt, or texture, paint has been added to the trace paint of the previous panel and the perspec-

64

Fig. 4-18 Painted window demonstrating effectiveness of paint used minimally but directly complementing the design. (*Courtesy Susie Creamcheese, Las Vegas, Nevada*)

tive is in order. Starting with the sea, we note the waves boiling round the vessel in a fury of motion imparted by the textured effect of the matt. Such paint is applied in one of two ways— either as a second firing after the trace paint or directly over and parallel to the unfired trace paint so long as extreme care is taken not to smudge it. Both paints may then be cured with one firing. (See *How to Work in Stained Glass* for details on firing.)

There are three other areas that have profited from the depth added by texture: the hull, the sails and the sky. Streaks of matt paint add immensity to the sky compared to the previous two panels and locate the ship in space by closing off the horizon. Within specific borders, the vessel crests the billows, its forefoot wave splashing within its lead line. It's the same lead line that was present in the first panel; compare the difference. The sails billow forth creased with the strain of wind and weather. Their paint, fine-lined by a blender brush, and the hull shows what can be wrought with the brush or stick lighting techniques discussed previously.

In these three panels, you can see the fulfillment of the notion that stained glass profits from painted detail as long as the particulars do not overwhelm the glass concept. Every panel that incorporates paint must subscribe to this rule if the elements of painting and glass, so fiercely independent, are to combine with any chance of success.

In the preceding panels, there is illustrative proof how superbly paint and glass can relate and combine, providing a fulfillment more spectacular than either could effect alone (see Figs. 4-18 and 4-19).

Fig. 4-19 Painted and jeweled window balancing the glass design perfectly. This and the example in Figure 4-18 are two of the most tastefully painted windows we've recently come across. (*Courtesy Susie Creamcheese, Las Vegas, Nevada*)

# Chapter 5

# LAMPS—
# MORE LIGHT ON
# THE SUBJECT

## MAKING LAMPS WITH MOLDS

A number of molds for lamps have recently appeared on the scene, making it much simpler for the craftsman to acquire a shape to his liking than has ever been possible previously. A great step forward was the fabrication of such molds out of interlocking (more or less) pieces of Styrofoam®; some companies go so far as to present designs inked right on the surface (see Fig. 5-1). It is not necessary in such instances to have more than one panel of a lamp to fabricate the entire shape, as long as you know how many panels you must make for the whole to go together.

For many craftsmen, this type of thing is soon outgrown. It becomes rather like painting by number; when creative design is limited by pre-set guidelines, this can be a bore. All the same, rock maple molds are expensive to have made. You can make your own molds of other material if you want to take the time and apply as much thought to them as you would to the lamp itself. Two methods of doing this follow.

### The Wooden Mold

The completed mold shown in Figure 5-2 is 22″ in diameter and 11″ high. The particular shade that was made from it includes four clusters of red grapes (eighteen grapes per cluster) and four clusters of purple grapes (eight per cluster). These are bounded by green leaves with a caramel/white background.

A power wood-turning lathe must be used to make the mold. However, to employ a wood lathe of the size capable of working a solid piece of wood to these measurements calls for considerable expense. The question arose, could a small wood lathe be used? Although the individual who made this mold eventually purchased his own lathe, small wood lathes are not hard to locate;

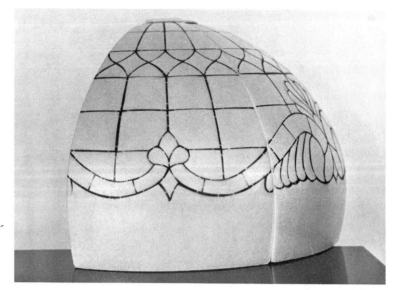

Fig. 5-1 A commercial Styrofoam mold. The design is screened onto the surface. (*Courtesy, the H. L. Worden Company*)

many schools that give woodworking classes have one and, if you are part of the community, may do the job for you as a favor. But still the weight of wood involved for these dimensions would provide more vibration than such a lathe could take.

Accordingly, the lower mold was first divided into four sections and was made one section at a time (see Fig. 5-2). Each of the four sections is itself composed of sections of 1″ stock glued together, starting at the base. As each section was completed, it was glued onto the section below, the mold being built up into the typical conical shape. The wood used is 1″ clear pine stock and it is glued with a white glue, such Elmer's® , which will hold the laminations well.

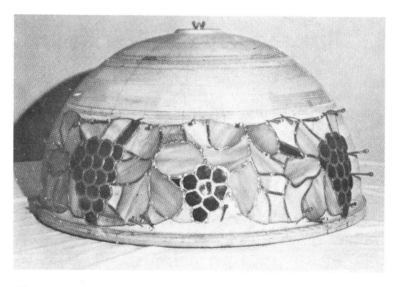

Fig. 5-2 A wooden mold. (*Courtesy, A. Grotzky*)

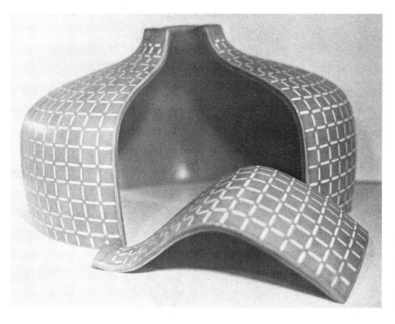

Fig. 5-3 Lamps Ltd. presents a new, heavy plastic interlocking mold which comes with or without an impressed design. This mold is practically indestructible. You can solder against it, even nail into it, without disrupting its surface. From just one section, the entire glass circle can be calculated. The entire mold is also sold and the pieces hold firmly together.

Any or all of the top three sections of the mold can be removed and other sections made to replace them so as to change the shape of the basic 22″ diameter form to any other shape desired. Each section is bolted to the section below with guide pins and a wing nut securing the top section. There are white rubber "nail in" type bumpers on the bottom of the form so it may be placed on a good desk or table to be worked on without damage to the surface. When the shade being worked on is completed, the nail holes that remain in the wood from the supporting nails can be filled in with plastic wood, or they can be left alone. If plastic wood is used, sand carefully over the holes when they are dry and you are ready for your next lamp.

You can also make a jig, if you wish, that will hold this type of mold, or you can buy one (see Sources of Supply listing). Such a jig will allow the shade and mold to tip up to a full 360°. Thus, when you are soldering, you can work on a level which prevents the molten solder from running down the sides of the piece in progress—this saves time and solder.

Figure 5-3 shows a new type of mold now available.

### The Styrofoam Mold

The same concept described above can be realized in Styrofoam, and the process is actually simpler since no lathe is needed. First, you must acquire sheets of Styrofoam from your local hobby or craft store. The thickness and width used should be the maximum you can buy. Neither measurement will exactly serve your purpose and you will have to put a number of these sheets together.

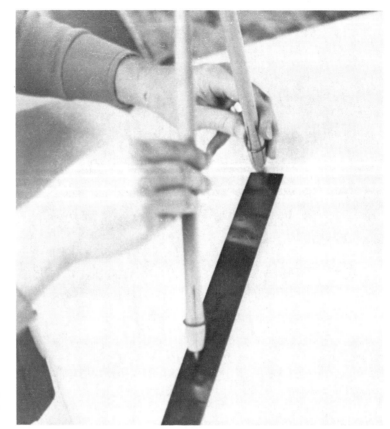

Fig. 5-4 Making a Styrofoam mold. The initial measurement.

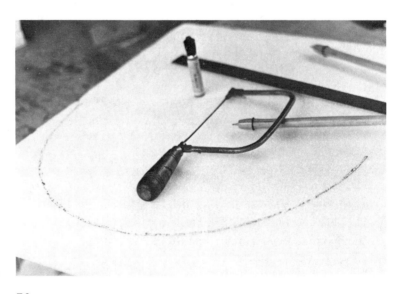

Fig. 5-5 The semicircle marked and ready to be cut.

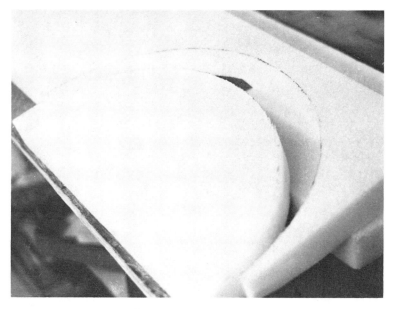

Fig. 5-6   The first semicircle
cut out.

Figure 5-4 shows the initial measurement across a piece of
Styrofoam to find the radius of the diameter you are planning for
your lamp. Once the radius is established, a large compass is used
to inscribe a semicircle. This must be clearly marked with a felt
tip pen after it has been inscribed into the Styrofoam (see Fig.
5-5).

Figure 5-6 shows the semicircle cut from the Styrofoam. It
must be cut along the inscribed line as precisely as possible. You
can use a hand coping saw, but we find more exact results with
an electric jigsaw. Either way, you will kick up a lot of Styrofoam
dust which is not healthy to breathe. A handkerchief around the
mouth and nose should be used to keep this dust out of the lungs.

Figure 5-7 shows two pieces of the semicircle which were glued
together and are now being trimmed with an electric jigsaw. Any

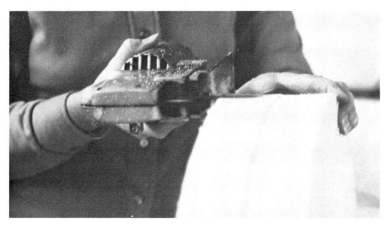

Fig. 5-7   Smoothing the
mold surface with an electric
jigsaw.

71

Fig. 5-8 Three layers of Styrofoam, the top piece of a different thickness than the other two, go into making this particular mold.

glue will work on Styrofoam; just make certain you have the edges exact before you stick them together. They are difficult to separate afterwards, and you can tear the piece trying to even edges after gluing.

Figure 5-8 gives an idea how many pieces of Styrofoam, and of what thicknesses, were necessary for the project under consideration—a small-pieced lamp skirt 6″ high.

With the three pieces of Styrofoam shown in Figure 5-8 now

Fig. 5-9 The paper guide is placed over the mold.

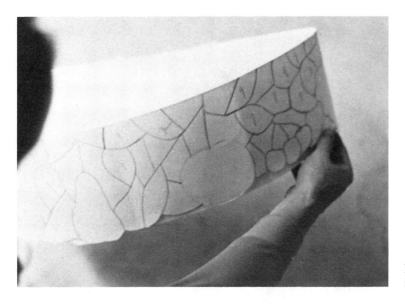

Fig. 5-10   The paper pattern
is snugged into place.

glued together, the pattern is placed over them to show exactly
where each piece of glass is to go (see Fig. 5-9). Since the paper
pattern is circular—and we purposely made it this way to acquire
the exact dimension of each piece of glass around the total design—it must be doubled up against the straight back of the
semicircular mold (see Fig. 5-10).

In Figure 5-11, with the mold and pattern in position, the first
pieces of glass are put into place. These have already been foiled
and are now to be tacked together. A great advantage to using
the semicircular mold is that you have a flat, smooth surface

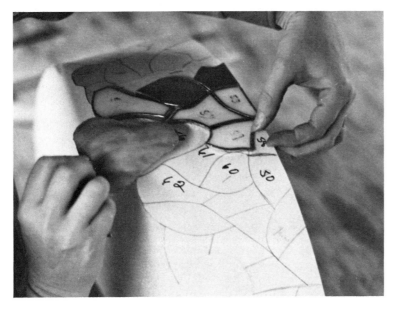

Fig. 5-11   The pieces of glass
are foiled into place atop the
pattern.

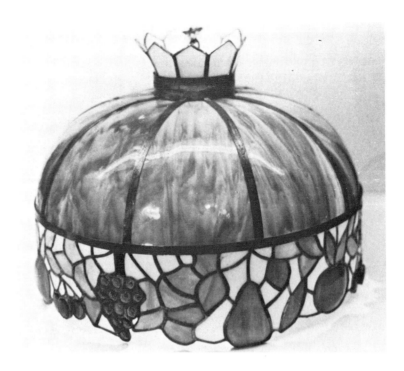

Fig. 5-12 Completed lamp made from Styrofoam mold. (Collection of Paula Silverman)

which you can stand upright on your work surface, allowing straight down soldering. As you begin to work around the curvature, supports can be placed beneath the bottom surface to lift the section of the mold you are working to a basically horizontal position. This eliminates the need of a jig of any sort.

The full curvature of the mold must be used twice; the pieces of glass forming the bridge between the two halves are put into place after the two pieces come off the mold. The completed lamp made from this Styrofoam mold is shown in Figure 5-12.

REPRODUCING PAINTED PATTERNS

Many old lampshades, have lovely painted panels (see Fig. 5-13.) You will often find sound frames with only a few of these panels left. There are three ways you can remedy this: refill the frame by replacing all the panels with new, unpainted panels; make every painted panel an alternate to a new, unpainted one (if enough original painted panels survive); or try to re-paint a panel as closely allied to the others as possible. This can be a difficult job where colors are involved; you will never match them unless you are very lucky. Matching colors won't be a problem where only a black trace background is required; here you may be able to get away with a transfer.

Let us take an example of this process with the shade shown in Figure 5-14. One panel of this lamp—a duplicate of the one to the left—was missing. Was it worth going to the trouble to re-

74

Fig. 5-13   A typical painted lamp panel.

place it? The base shown in Figure 5-15 was in good shape, so it seemed a shame not to take the time to make the shade as perfect as possible—especially since the designs were black paint silhouettes.

We were fortunate to have a piece of the same type of glass—really an old commercial glass, not an art glass. The ridging required us to paint on the inner, smooth surface. Painting on a ridged surface is difficult by hand. When these panels

Fig. 5-14   This shade has a broken panel which we will attempt to match. Note the ridged glass surfaces.

Fig. 5-15 The base of the
shade in Figure 5-14.

were done commercially, they were silk screened onto the glass
and then baked at the same time the glass was being bent to
shape. In cases where several panels are missing from very good
frames, we use photographic silk screening to make the stencil
and transfer the designs in this fashion. Our purpose here is to
show how to do it by hand.

*Drawing the Picture*

Wrap a piece of very strong, thin paper (such as regular tracing
paper) around an existing painted panel. Attach the edges of
paper to the glass with cellophane tape. Hold the panel firmly
over the light table and with a sharp pencil trace the outlines of
the drawing's major elements piece by piece. In this case, we first
do the dancing woman, then the fence and some of the bushes.
The smaller incidentals can be filled in freehand by copying
around the transferred portions; if this part is a little inexact, no
one will notice.

When you have traced the design, remove the paper from the
panel and transfer the design from the thin paper to a piece of
pattern paper or stencil paper. The lines now must be made firm

76

with another pencil and extensive measurements taken to make sure that what you have on paper conforms as closely as possible to what is on the original piece of glass.

When you are satisfied that this is the case, cut around the lines with a stencil knife and remove the core of the drawing from the paper (Fig. 5-16). You will note in this figure that two inner areas—the triangular space between the elbows, knees and belly and the smaller triangle separating the arms—have come away with the paper, leaving only a broad silhouette opening in the paper. These two triangles must now be carefully cut out of the center core and safely placed aside. The rest of the paper figure is not needed.

Now, wrap the pattern paper around the new panel, matching the hole representing the figure to its position on the old panel (see Fig. 5-17). This heavier paper will not adhere to the glass bend as well as the tracing paper, but you must position it as flat against the glass as possible. This is easier, of course, with straight panel lamps. In areas where the paper insists on bulging away from the glass, a small dollop of rubber cement behind it may help. It can take as long as one-half to three-quarters of an hour to get the paper settled so that the opening is positioned correctly and the paper is absolutely flat. Now the two triangles of paper previously cut out are placed in position on the glass with rubber cement. You might want to rubber cement the edges of the central opening as well, since it is imperative that no paint flows beneath this area.

With all pieces in place, the painting is now accomplished by the simple expedient of filling in the hole. You can smear the paint in place as long as the consistency is proper. After the

Fig. 5-16 The template with the central core containing two triangles of paper that must be replaced on the surface to be painted.

77

Fig. 5-17 The template wrapped on the glass to be painted. It is not yet flat enough to the surface for paint to be applied.

Fig. 5-18 The completed panel.

paint dries, pry or tear or lift the paper away, being careful not to chip the paint. This leaves you with a negative image of the hole in the paper. If any small amount of paint has managed to get under the margins, you can clean it out with a sharp stick, but try not to allow this to happen. If you get careless, thinking that you are going to clean such dribblings of paint up anyway, you'll get so much seepage you may lose the entire figure. The more care you take, the better the project will turn out.

Each area of painting you transfer from the master panel must be treated this way. Don't rush. It can take hours to transfer the simplest painting in this fashion, mostly because of fussing with the papers. However, the less you leave to be done freehand, the more exact your duplicate will look. Figure 5-18 shows our transferred panel for this project.

*Firing the Panel*

Firing a panel for painting should not be done at the same time as firing for bending (see *How to Work in Stained Glass* for firing techniques). The higher heat required for bending a panel could fry the paint. So, bend your glass first and paint later.

Refiring a bent panel for a painted surface involves placing the panel back on the mold which served for the bending originally. Where painting appears on the inner surface, this is not possible since the uncured paint would rest against the mold surface. Instead, we must make a new mold out of clay.

This is formed by pressing the glass bend into the clay with the inner surface upward. It isn't a difficult procedure since the mold is only supportive and we will not be raising the temperature high enough to sag the glass. All the same, if we do not support the curvature, even at this relatively low temperature of 1100°–1150°F, some sagging might take place—enough to pro-

Fig. 5-19 The Chunk Lamp (*Courtesy Rik Heidloff*)

79

vide an inexactness which will prevent the curved panel from fitting back into the frame. Better to be safe than sorry.

MAKING A LAMP WITHOUT A MOLD

*The Chunk Lampshade*

Figure 5-19 shows what may happen to a shade composed of chunk glass rather than flat pieces. It acquires more of a sculptured effect rather than a linear quality and each chunk becomes a miniature refractory organ fragmenting light within its surface. This provides a dramatic effect.

In the chunk shade shown, you will note that the entire top tier and part of the second tier are composed of routinely cut glass pieces. A mold isn't needed for this type shade since the basic shape is formed by the first tier of flat pieces. The chunks are foiled together; no flat glass lies beneath them.

# Chapter 6

# BOXES—
# FLIPPING
# YOUR
# LID

Stained glass boxes have intrigued workers in the craft from Tiffany on down (see Fig. 6-1). While Tiffany incorporated stained glass and bronze into many of his boxes, he utilized metal filigree as the main feature with glass as the background. Present workers tend to sculpt their boxes directly from the glass itself. One such designer is Elliott Wiener whose work we will show in this chapter.

DESIGNING

It is unfortunate that the concept of a box, basically rectangles or squares enclosing a space of some sort, appears so simple to many workers. As we try to show throughout the course of this book, simplicity is one of the most difficult considerations to design; it should be implied rather than expressed and generally involves a lot of circumlocutions instead of a straight path. Truly simple designs are not very interesting. Designing a box should be easy: four sides, a top and a bottom.

This straightforward proposal is put to some use in Figure 6-2 which demonstrates how the most obvious idea can evolve into something quite unique. This clutch of boxes has been made into a sculptured piece. From a design standpoint, one box of this nature is nothing; two or three not much more; the whole concept, however, is everything. So for those whose idea of a box stops with the form itself, the design is a dead end no matter how many pieces of glass you cut up for sides and top. The consideration of the box as a spatial object with possibilities within and without its own requirements is something else again. We will try to demonstrate this in the following examples.

81

Fig. 6-1 Two Tiffany boxes; the left hand one is an ink-well, the right a jewelry box.

Fig. 6-2 Design with boxes of stained glass.

*Making an Inlaid Lid: The Eagle Box*

The sides of the box shown here in Figure 6-3 are built of three glass strips foiled together in straight lines so as not to detract from the emblem at the top. This surface demonstrates an inlaid, foiled eagle which is attached to the bordering lines at the two sides and the bottom. Two additional lines extend from the corners of the central panel to the lower body of the eagle. The right and left sides of the box are decorated with brass beading which brings these portions to the level of the beading over the eagle.

There are over fifty pieces of glass within the eagle itself. Each has been cut precisely to shape and foiled into place. Note that the design chosen provides its own limits; it is narrowly rectangular and has to fit within a central panel rather than take up the

82

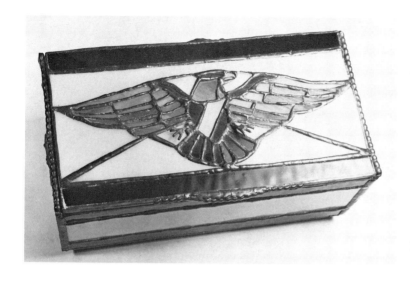

Fig. 6-3 The Eagle Box.
(*Courtesy Elliott Wiener*)

entire lid surface. This background panel is white opalescent glass which throws off the colors of the eagle quite nicely.

There are two ways of making inlaid designs on boxes. The first is to make a "false" inlay by making a panel, of whatever design, and utilizing it as the top of the box. In this instance, when the hinged lid is picked up, the entire design will be seen from the underside of the lid.

We prefer a "true" inlay onto an existing surface. Here the top lid is provided and hinged as a separate piece of glass; on its surface, the design is foiled together and soldered. Only the top surface of the design is seen; the design cannot be seen when the lid is open. This, we feel, gives a more substantial effect.

*Making a Three-Dimensional Lid: The Spider Box*

A novel idea, the box shown in Figure 6-4 shows a spider made of glass globs and copper wire crawling over the raised, triangular webbing which forms the top of the piece. The effect is pleasing, due to both the creative effort involved and the shape chosen. A flat lid would have been less intriguing. The web lines leading from the corners to the center accentuate their prowling occupant as well as the gradual elevation of the lid. Note the number of break lines in the lid alone. A few blades of grass and a mushroom overlie the sides; this design is effective as background to the spider and they stand out from the small panels as an emphatic foreground.

Not the least of the challenges inherent in this project is making the lid functional as well as decorative. In effect, each of the four lower sides of the lid is a narrow triangle with the base lines meeting the sides of the box proper. These must be precisely cut; any discrepancy at all will show. The hinging is placed

83

Fig. 6-4 The Spider Box, the Trunk Box, the Chinese Box. (*Courtesy Elliott Wiener*)

across from our view at the level of this lower straight line; the lifting tab is soldered to the front which is facing us. It all makes for a heavier lid than usual, but the outside is so interesting how often do you expect to look within?

*Making a Curved Lid: The Trunk Box*

The basic shape of this box, shown in Figure 6-4, is a high, rectangle. The lower rim, front and back are separate pieces of glass. White opalescent is used for these sides. The back contains only the hinges; we like to use strapping on the back as well as the front to give the impression of this material going all around the trunk. It looks more realistic.

84

These straps, in the front especially, are meant to appear as though they bind the lid down. You can use brass banding for straps; make sure you get a design that realistically approaches leather. Many lamp fixtures stores now carry a number of different styles of this material or will order it for you. Several feet of different style brass banding is always good to have in your workshop; as you will see in the course of this book, we make use of this material often.

Run a piece of banding from top to bottom on each side of the front surface. Then from the top solder line, run another piece one-half or three-quarters of the way down directly on top of the first piece. Clip the ends to a triangular point and make sure both strips are lying flat. For a buckle you can modify a lamp hook, use copper wire bent to shape or a piece of lead came that can be twisted to shape. The buckle can be open in the back; solder these open ends to the back strip of banding, using copper foil wraps on the ends if they don't take solder. If you are going to place straps on the back as well, you need to place the banding so that it indicates a continuation of what is going on in front. Of course, if you want your trunk to look the same from either direction, you can exactly duplicate the front on this back surface as well, by adding matching buckles.

The lock can be made of another piece of brass banding cut to a roughly oval shape; solder a loop to the top to represent the hasp. This can be a small piece of solder itself bent to shape with its ends attached to the brass plate. It is important to the character of the piece that this lock should appear a massive affair; you might whack your brass (or lead plate if you wish) with a hammer to give it a long-suffering aged look.

Quite effective for the strapping is the use of actual straps or thin belts cut to size. You can utilize buckles and all. The cut ends, wrapped with foil, will solder to the lead lines of the box, giving a natural appearance.

The two side pieces of the rectangle can be made in one of two ways. You can, as was done here, use the same opalescent white as you did for the front and back and overlay it with a wide strip of brass banding that has a decorative open area through which the glass will show. This banding spans the entire length of either side. In the middle, place a brass handle which you can make from thin banding.

Another method of changing the rhythm of the four-square appearance is to use opalescent glass on the sides dissimilar to the front and back with the roughest surface you can find. A long brass handle spanning the width is soldered to the seams half way down the side of the box.

The lid is made of twelve long, fairly thin strips to give it the bent appearance. This bend is guided by the two side pieces which are cut as semicircles with the flat base meeting the tops of the basic rectangular-shaped sides. Needless to say, both these side pieces must be cut the same. Once they are ready, support them on the table in upright position and solder the top center strip of glass into place. This will form a strut across, enabling you to solder the remainder of the strips with little difficulty. Foil is used throughout. Solder a handle to the top and you are ready for hinging.

*Making a Recessed Lid: The Chinese Box*

Here's another inlaid design, shown in Figure 6-4, which this time takes up the entire lid. As discussed earlier, lettering makes very pleasing patterns in glass. Here's a foreign murmur quite distinguished design-wise. The focal point is the lid—an unhinged, lift-off type which when closed fits flush with the right and left sides of the box. The lettering shows up well in green opalescent; the background is our favorite white opal. For the sides, a caramel opal was brought into play. Here you can add an extra flip of the imagination by making this a three-tiered affair. Not only can the box be opened by lifting the lid, but the entire top-half portion can be removed. This is accomplished by using two pieces for each of the four sides; the flow of the pieced metal design hides this break and supports the two sections. This is accomplished by using the same thin banding of brass or lead as shown for a one-piece box, but extend it across the top edge of the bottom half portion of the box. When we pick up the top portion, we will have a series of lead or brass spikes remaining as a little fence around the lower shelf onto which the top can easily be replaced. It is not convenient to do this with the lid; the two side supports here are sufficient, although the brass design is carried out beneath it to make it seem more natural in the center.

*Making a Cameo Effect: The Fish Box*

The lid design, shown in Figure 6-5, and the clasp are extremely ornate. An attempt is being made to give a cameo effect via an oval border. This is placed in a background of roughly soldered copper bordered with some of our omnipresent brass beading.

The basic lines of the design flow from top to bottom, carrying the eye along the narrow depth of the box. The fish adds an overlay effect. Its body is a large glass glob, melding at its circumferences into fins, tail and mouth, strongly indicated by solder lines and moderately by change in glass color. This lid is un-

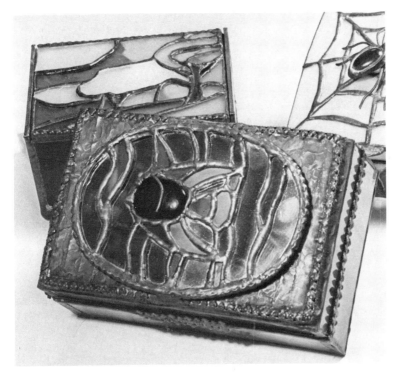

hinged and the covering of copper is supported by foiling around the top glass edges.

Standing out most strongly in the design, and contributing more than any other element to the cameo effect, is the oval border. This can be made of lead came built up with solder or a high brass beading. It should rise a good ½″ above the lid surface.

### Making a Pictorial Lid: The Country Box

Our next example in Figure 6-5 shows a simple scene almost like a watercolor. Again this is an inlay; but unlike the other boxes shown, there is no background for the lid surface per se. The entire surface is pictorial. Fairly large sweeps of glass are used and the effect is soothing. This is a quiet box; the restfulness of its cover is emphasized by the plainness of its sides. It shows what can be accomplished by a good, uncluttered design. The lid will be hinged for practicality, but for purposes of completion, it rests between two sides built up to its level.

### Making a Sculptured Effect: Jack-in-the-Box

The box in Figure 6-6 is secondary to what's inside it. This box neither opens nor closes; it is, in fact, a very plain affair, aside from its little music box, purposely made to be a background

87

Fig. 6-6 Jack-In-The-Box.
(*Courtesy Elliott Wiener*)

item. The Jack is detailed and must be made in perspective to look as though he could fit in the box. We show him a little on a slant, which is how these things pop out at you, and very pleased to have scared you to death. In such a case, you may end up in a box yourself.

HINGING

A main problem in fabricating boxes is the hinges—how to place them, how to maintain their function, how to keep them sturdy. As we have pointed out, it is not necessary to hinge every box. Lids can be slid, lifted, rotated, fixed or can even be absent, depending on the effect desired. But if you're going to use a hinge, it might be well to keep the following guidelines in mind.

Small brass hinges, available in hardware stores, are sturdy and will maintain a linear area at least three times their length. That is to say, a 2″ hinge will support a lid 6″ long if placed in its center. This is a good rule of thumb to use when purchasing hinges for your particular size lid. Make sure the hinges are solid brass and are not just plated, or they won't solder. Galvanized steel hinges will also work. We try to stay away from piano hinges (long, continuous hinges that cover an entire surface) since they are more work, but they can be used if you want to spend the extra time. Two well-placed small hinges of the proper dimension will do the same job.

### Maintaining Hinge Function

The most frustrating problem with hinge function is dropping flux or solder in the workings. Solder will show up right away as an instant freeze; flux and flux residues will take longer. The end result is immobility of the hinge and, if you try to force it, perhaps cracking of the glass; or at the least a pulling away of the hinge from its base. The way to eliminate this is to be careful during the soldering process not to drip flux or solder about. Tin the flanges of the hinge carefully, holding it flat down on the table; stay away from the joint. This pre-tinning will make the soldering operation easier when the lid and box are being attached. People tend to forget brass gets hot during soldering; dropping the hinge doesn't help keep it clean. Hold the hinge with a small pliers when attaching it. A drop of oil in the joint will keep its operation smooth.

### Placing the Hinge

The solidity of the hinge joint and, therefore of the entire lid, depends on how you place the hinges. Since we deal mostly with copper foil in making boxes, the glass edging though beaded with solder is not strong enough to hold a hinge securely. The brass will solder to the foil all right; but if there is the slightest strain, the foil will pull away from the glass. There are several ways to overcome this.

*Using Glue*   Our old friend, Duco Cement comes in handy here. Coat the inner flange of each hinge with the glue so it will adhere to the glass itself; then solder that portion that corresponds to the copper foil edge. Now you have a double bond.

*Building up the Box Edge*   It's difficult to do this to just one edge; you really have to match it up with the other three. You can get away with it if you've allowed for it in the cutting, however. By making the hinging side of the box a trifle smaller than the other sides, you can fill in with lead came. The came may not adhere well enough to the glass itself to avoid being pulled off by the weight of the lid; but if you drop some glue into the channel, it will become sturdy. Now you can solder your hinges in place.

*Building up the Surface*   You can stretch extra bands of copper foil over the surface just below the edge to be hinged. This will permit more of the soldering area to catch the flanges of the hinge. This process can be done artistically; indeed small lead castings can be glued into place on the glass and the hinges soldered to them.

*Designing Break Lines*   In this instance, the back side of the box is specifically broken with lead lines to catch the hinges. Vertical lines would be obviously practical, but you'll want to provide enough of a design to offset the obvious. Done with taste, you can accomplish beauty and function. Who can ask for anything more?

There are other methods for maintaining hinge stability but most of them are based on some function or combination of the ones above. Doubtless, guided by these, you will come up with the method or methods that work best for you.

# Chapter 7

# COMBINING GLASS WITH METAL AND WOOD

GLASS AND METAL

Use of metals such as copper, brass, galvanized tin and so forth in glass projects is common. It is not so common to use glass within essentially metal projects. Here the metal is the primary consideration and glass secondary, enhancing or re-evaluating the design. Of the three projects shown in this chapter, not one was conceived with stained glass in mind. Each was the idea of a craftsman hoping to achieve an effect based on spatial representation of the metal alone. Let us give you an idea of the difference between the two types of thinking.

*The Sled*

Figure 7-1 shows a typical balance between stained glass and metal. Here the concept is obviously glass; the brass runner, taken from a wide lamp banding cut to size and design, is a finishing touch. True it is a novel and provocative finishing touch, but as such it is obviously not the area from which the conception sprung. The sled was made first, the packages and leaves added to it and then imagination took hold and demanded ornate runners to close in the project. The brass banding alone does not indicate a sled; the stained glass portion does. Together they form an interesting totality.

In this chapter, we want to propose the following question: suppose all you had to start with was a piece of metal, in this case the brass runner. Which way would you travel? Would it suggest a sled to you? What would you do with it? What we have done, starting with completed metal objects, is discussed in the following pages.

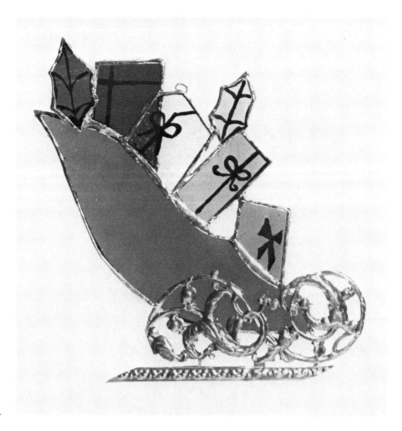

Fig. 7-1 The Sled.

### The Star

The composition shown in Figure 7-2 is made of steel nails braised together, and is a metal sculpture complete in itself. Yet to us, looking at it glassily so to speak, it's still incomplete. Would stained glass enhance its effect? Not in the outer portion; that would throw it off balance. But the inner figure; that's something else—it looks rather like a star. Let us enhance this proposal by placing glass within the open spaces. We will not use the same color of glass all the way through but we'll alternate colors. Now it remains to decide which colors to use? White is always a safe, neutral color and blue stands out nicely with metal; both opalescent, of course.

Figure 7-3 shows the completed effect, using this glass and these colors alternately around the central figure. Design-wise the emptiness of the center which bothered us before is gone. The piece has a sparkle and character that it formerly lacked. And, most important, the glass has not in any way detracted from the basic metallic essence of this composition.

The technique involved was painstaking. Because these steel nails will not solder, we had to wrap each surface with copper

92

Fig. 7-2 Nail sculpture awaiting stained glass. (*Courtesy L. M. Elting*)

foil. This wrapping must be tight. The glass was then cut to the proper dimensions by tracing the inner spaces against a piece of pattern paper and cutting to size. Copper foil was wrapped around the glass and each piece soldered into place against the existing rim of foil. For perhaps three hours' work, you have a figuration in two craft modalities.

## The Fierce Fish

A slightly more complicated imaginative query was posed by Figure 7-4. What does this look like to you? There are several possibilities: a rocket, a space module, a fish, a turtle. At first we were going to use it as a turtle with the left square as the head and the back triangle the tail and part of the central shell. We decided, however, on the fish.

First we wrapped foil around *all* surfaces, because all surfaces will be soldered to glass. Although this piece is composed of brass bars curved and braised together, by the time we got to work they were oxidized and would not take solder well. We could have taken the time to clean them but since we were covering them with foil it wasn't necessary.

93

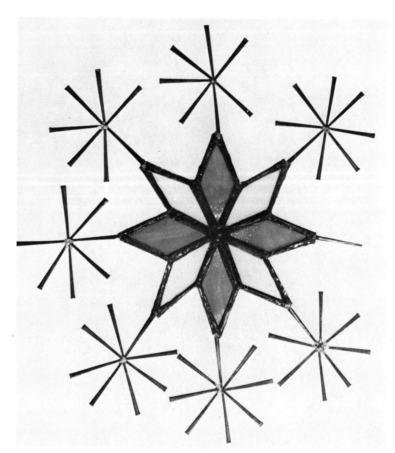

Fig. 7-3 The Star.

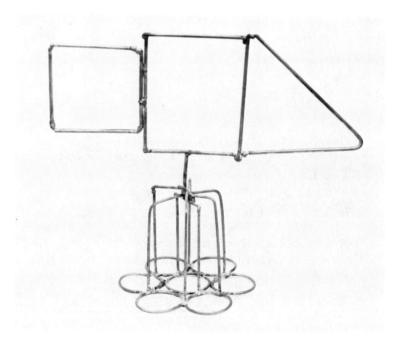

Fig. 7-4 Brass sculpture awaiting stained glass. (*Courtesy L. M. Elting*)

We next cut the three center pieces from opalescent glass, making sure we grozed back (with a grozing pliers) a small portion of the front triangle to represent the nose by a negative space. These pieces were foiled and soldered in place.

Our fish was beginning to take shape but the body looked blunt, unfinished and graceless. We decided to take some liberty with the original sculpture and add a tail. This would be a long triangle to balance the one in front and, to provide suppleness to the design, we placed it at an angle of 45° to the rest of the body. This made the fish appear to be swimming.

Our basic design was now complete, but a few finishing touches remained. The eye, a plastic one, seemed an obvious commitment, but even with that rolling in his head the fish appeared bland. Character was added by placing the lower jaw: a small piece of opalescent glass soldered at an angle to the lower front triangle border. Determination was provided by affixing teeth herein; these are the only pieces of white opalescent in the entire project and they certainly stand out. The dorsal fin balanced the lower jaw and gave us the fish silhouette we were after. The fish was now off the hook.

The stand was a little tricky and somehow it kept looking like legs—a notion we didn't like since it fought the sleekness of the design above. We decided to make it part of the scene by disguising it with miscellaneous debris from the ocean. Figure 7-5 shows our use of glass chunks with the fish swimming over them. Coral could also have been used.

Fig. 7-5 The Fierce Fish. (See color section)

*The Trellis*

This was the most difficult of the proposals so far. We were again given a two-dimensional abstract nail sculpture as shown in Figure 7-6. For some reason, the concept of a trellis leaped instantly to mind. Whereas in both the first and second projects, we utilized glass within the borders given, now we were going to weave it betwixt and between. This would not only provide a three-dimensional result, it would make the metallic element more integral to this composition than in either of the other designs.

The first thing we had to do was decide on a design complementary to the nail pattern. The sinuosity of a vine suggested itself, partly because we wanted a garden scene, mostly because our nail sculpture was so angular. Between the curvature of the vine behind and the rigidity of the trellis in front, we would have flowers. So much for the first flicker of thought. We set about designing the vine out of lead came; and when we had what we wanted, we matched it up against the trellis for size. It was not meant to overpower the trellis, but it had to state its purpose. At those spots where the trellis directly overlaid the vine, easily found by placing the one directly on the other temporarily, we made marks for copper stems to be placed. This process is seen in Figure 7-7. Since the steel nails, as usual, do not solder, a small piece of copper foil was wrapped at these joints with two inches

Fig. 7-6 Nail sculpture awaiting stained glass. (*Courtesy L. M. Elting*)

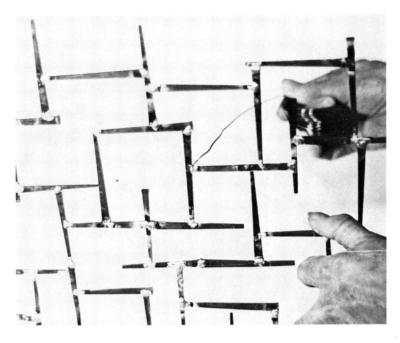

Fig. 7-7 Supporting wires
placed for the stained glass
background.

of wire run straight back. The other end of this wire was to be soldered to the lead vine.

The end result was almost box-like. The trellis was the front, the vine the back and tinned wire held them apart. In the space between flowers wandered.

Having gotten this much decided, we had to determine what kind of flowers to grow. We decided on tulips in various stages of bloom. A determination of how these would look against the trellis was necessary. The size of the flowers was very important. They had to be large enough to be emphatic but still submit to the forcefulness of the trellis without masking the vine. We decided their presence would be emphasized not so much by size but by position and shape. Having some of them made of bent glass would call attention to them and we felt that at least one of them should be wandering *through* the trellis. One or two leaves would break the monotony of the flowers so we cut some from old bent panels (see Chap. 3). Finally we felt that at least one of the flowers should not be a tulip for a bit of variety and for an added point of interest in the design.

All of the above represents a lot of designing in a small space (about 10″ high by 12″ wide). Yet if you look at Figure 7-8, I think you will agree we got away with it very nicely. Part of the reason for this was our use of space; not only side to side but front to back. The other reason is the trellis itself which flickers in and out of vision, depending on whether the eye is examining

97

Fig. 7-8 The Trellis. (See color section)

background or foreground. The only reason it does this is because the linear quality of background and foreground are so different that neither gets in the other's way. Imagine how confusing the whole thing would appear if the vine were angular like the trellis, or if the flowers were larger or smaller, or if there were more of them.

In three-dimensional designing, it is good to be aware that hints of things can be more powerful than the actualities. Note the stem of the vine, for example. This is cut short purposely; yet the eye goes automatically to it, led there by the curved pathways of the vine. There is no reason to make the stem longer; it would interfere with the bottom lines of the trellis. The only possible reason for extending it would be to place another flower in that area; obviously this would be of no use.

The effectiveness of spatial placement in this type of designing has been spoken of briefly but one more mention is due. Note that the majority of the flowers go off to the right and only two go to the left, and the lower of these is not essential to the balance. What balances this mass of right-handed growth is the upper left flower because of its foreground thrust. It comes through the trellis at us. This does not show up in the picture as well as we would like, but when viewing the actual object it is most apparent. Since this flower is closer to the eye, it more than compensates for a cluster further back. It's kind of like a bird in the hand being worth two in the bush. Now there's an idea for a project in metal.

## GLASS AND WOOD

We are all familiar with the use of wood and glass for shutters, doors and windows; but here wood is combined with glass as a part of the conception and not merely as a border.

### Spider Web Designs

Figure 7-9 shows an unusual example of how glass can be made to work with wood. The centrally located web is suspended from the four corners of the wooden frame and the spider hangs from the web. The irregular outline formed by the wood adds a natural setting where such a web might be found. Well, perhaps not exactly such a web since few spiders except Charlotte know how to spell.

The words "Some Judith" appear across the surface of the web—a spun tribute to the daughter of the craftsman. The spider

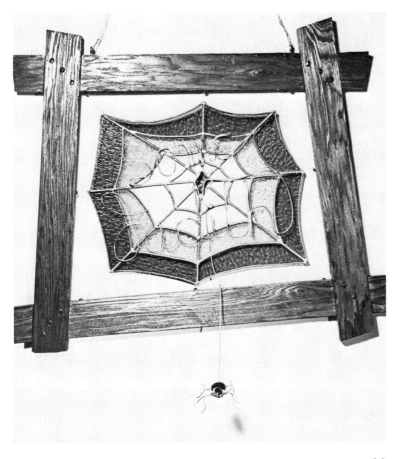

Fig. 7-9 Spider web with wood. (*Courtesy B. Laxer*)

99

Fig. 7-10 Design for a spider window.

is made of glass globs with copper wire legs; a heavier wire is used for the message. The web is a fairly simple affair of four irregular glass layers from a central core of basically regular spokes.

A more complicated design for a spider and her web is shown in Figure 7-10. This was a commission for an attic window of this overall shape. It was decided that such a dramatic and unusual concept would appropriately set off this area of the house.

The web was to be the lower portion of the panel attached to the bottom of the window, running to surrounding trees. The background would be sky and leaves from the trees. The spider, made from old Heidt Jewels (no longer available though similar ones can be bought in hobby or craft stores), was to be three-dimensional attached to a lead line by a strand of webbing, actually wire.

Difficulties in design here were to make the spider large enough to be glimpsed from below but not disproportionate to the web. We had to decide whether or not to make the webbing

Fig. 7-11 The spider window completed. (See color section)

100

extend over the entire window, but we felt this would be monotonous.

Figure 7-11 shows how this design worked out. A clear crackle glass was used for the web. This glass has a web-like texture of its own and it also allows the colors of the spider to show through. Opalescent glass was used for the sky and the tree limb on the left was double-glazed brown cathedral, streaky glass. The leaves are old pressed jewels. The entire window was foiled and no reinforcing was needed.

# 8 Chapter

# NOVELTY
# TECHNIQUES

There is always a call for original decorative objects in any craft; in stained glass, the competition is intense. There is always room for the novel, well-crafted item that makes its statement in a good natured fashion. We want to present a few of these, each of which embodies a technique or two you might find worthwhile.

OPEN BORDERS

Here, we are dealing with an edging of glass surrounding decorative empty space. Within this space is a design connected to the border not by a background of glass, but by chain, wire and wood—or the inner figure may present an element of its own design as a connecting link.

*Four Signs of the Zodiac*

*The Bull*  Figure 8-1 gives us Taurus done with stained glass and copper. The amount of painted detail is minimal; the horns have been cut from thin sheet copper. Copper wire gives the impression of back legs attached to stained glass haunches; the front legs are triangles reaching directly downward. The entire figure is framed within strips of stained glass that complement the shape of the bull.

The idea behind this is to make a series of zodiac signs in such frames; the frames need not be uniform to each other but must complete the figure within. Irregularly placed copper struts attach the inner subject to the outer border. Both border and foreground are so striking that the struts go all but unnoticed until the eye actually searches them out.

*The Crab*  Figure 8-2 shows another zodiac sign, Cancer, in its frame. The outer limit of glass combines the same number of pieces as the frame for the bull, but has been turned to accommo-

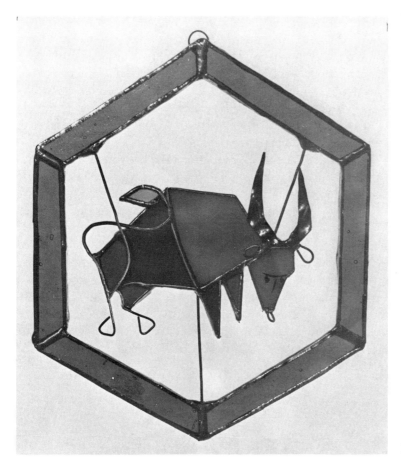

Fig. 8-1   The Bull.

Fig. 8-2   The Crab.

103

date the size and shape of the inner figure. The crab's secondary legs, that is the three inner ones on each side, are made of copper cut and folded to shape. The back legs and front claws are glass. The eyes are balls of solder which were soldered to the rim of foil surrounding the front of the body, and the antennae are coiled pieces of copper wire. The back two side legs have purposely been coiled over the border at this area to give the crab a sense of movement and impatience.

Three struts, evenly placed, attach the body within to the rim without. Since the main section of the crab is split down the center, this gives us the chance to bend the sides downward a little, allowing the center of the shell to appear raised.

*The Ram*   The ram in Figure 8-3 is another in this zodiac series. All these signs are amenable to glass and are highly prized by people with an astrological turn of mind. Aries is a bounding sort of fellow and we've indicated this by giving his front paws a very flexible turn, while his back paws are coiled in a circle represented by a jewel. His tailspread acts as a stabilizer and the circular frame we have put him in almost makes it appear as if he is jumping through it. Four small wires hold him in place and add to the free-floating effect.

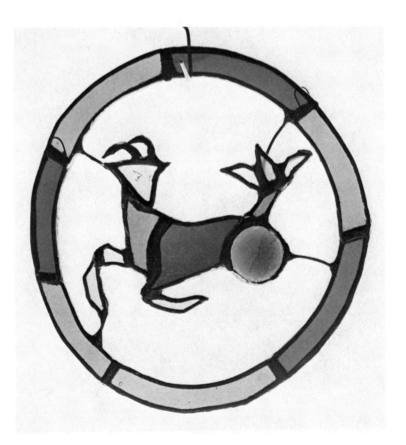

Fig. 8-3   The Ram.

Fig. 8-4 The Fish: sketch and beginning formation of the title in glass.

Other signs may require other border designs—from semicircles to triangles to trapezoids to squares. As long as there is some continuity between the inner subject and the outer frame, you will find you have an original result wherein one element provides the logic for the other.

*The Fish* Pisces, the fish, will be a larger display than those previously shown. You can see in Figure 8-4 that the glasswork will be more ornate. The name of the sign will be spelled out in glass and the fish itself will have a double image, with the lower figure in paler tones as though it's a reflection of the one above.

In Figure 8-5, you can see the top fish in glass. We have used mirror for the head and to this we glued a small glass jewel for the eye and soldered a piece of wire for the mouth. This is reflected in the mirror and forms a double image which adds depth to this thin line.

The curve of the tail has been changed from the one originally indicated in our design, though the spatial arrangement is basi-

105

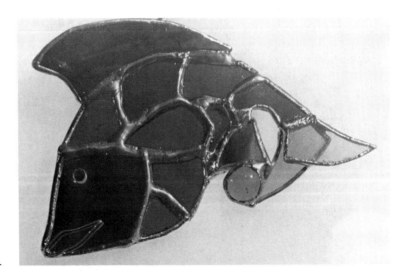

Fig. 8-5  The Fish in glass.

cally the same. The top fin is folded slightly forward and is a piece of lovely, streaky glass. The fish measures 5″ from nose to tail and 3″ at its widest portion. It will be placed in an open rectangular border to which each fish will be attached by decorative stiff wires, leading from the mouths as though they were hooked on a line. One fish alone makes a lovely pendant, and the reason it has yet to be placed in its intended design is that it has been constantly employed as such!

BOXES

This is a method of using straight line cuts in three-dimensional patterns. The result is to provide an enclosed space in some geometric shape or abstraction. Measurements must be accurate to keep these parallel cuts in line.

Fig. 8-6  Another practical but novel use of stained glass is for belt buckle designs.

Fig. 8-7 The Alphabet
Block. (*Courtesy Rik Heidloff*)

### The Alphabet

Here are two examples showing how items can be readily made utilizing designs from language. Figure 8-7 demonstrates an alphabet block. Facing us is a C; to the left is an A; every other surface contains a letter. Six small panels soldered together as a cube form the total project.

The novelty evolves from two elements: the pleasant sense of recognition—even nostalgia—that we get from the item, plus the amusing realization that even this can be accomplished in glass in a provocative fashion. The technique is simple—once you make sure all your lines are absolutely straight. If your block sags to one side or another, even a trifle, the entire effect is ruined. The alphabet blocks of our childhood had a solidity on which we still depend; the glass presentation must match up.

Lettering alone can provide forceful designs. In Figure 8-8 the letter A is done dimensionally in box formation, using lead came rather than foil to continue the strength inherent in the linear quality. You don't have to know how to draw to do interesting shapes in glass!

### The Closet

Utilization of the box technique provided the impetus for this endeavor shown in Figure 8-9. The rectangular box on end becomes a closet with an open door. To emphasize the ingenuity behind it, a suit of clothes, neatly foiled and pressed, hangs on the door, while another dimly lurks within. The whole joke is

Fig. 8-8 The letter A.
(*Courtesy Rik Heidloff*)

the suit of clothes; but the box-providing closet is the straight man behind it.

*The Whatsit Boxes*

Figure 8-10 presents layered boxes with a mirror on one end and the back ends of small bottles sticking out the other. A small owl seems to be caught in the lower box; actually this is a reflection from another part of the shop, but it demonstrates the magic that goes with this technique. One side of the box can be a wooden slab with holes drilled in to support the bottles, or a piece of glass to which half bottles must then be glued on a slight slant. It may not be a functional project, but it does make for a fascinating display. Haunt your local drugstore for small bottles; they must all be the same size.

This method encompasses a specific amount of open space within which some decorative motif may be placed. It is, of course, three-dimensional in nature.

### The Birdcage

Empty birdcages are not hard to find, so you may not have to go out and buy a new one. Friends may have these items in their attic. Although the idea is very simple, it is also effective. Figure 8-11 shows such a cage once more filled with feathered friends—even though the feathers are stained glass.

The two birds are simple, but you can get as decorative and ornate as you like. The size and number of birds depends on the size of the cage and also on whatever else you may want to add, such as three-dimensional trees, flowers and so forth. The more realistically you present your bird or birds, the greater the caged effect

Fig. 8-9   The Closet. (*Courtesy Rik Heidloff, photo by Rick Pawelka*)

Fig. 8-10 The Whatsit boxes.
(*Courtesy Glassart Studio*)

Fig. 8-11 Birds in a cage.
(*Courtesy Rik Heidloff, photo
by Rick Pawelka*)

will become. There might be a reason for the bird being caged; fierceness is a dramatic possibility. The cage acts as a three-dimensional border around the project, adding to or commenting on the action within—rather like the open border design we discussed previously in this chapter. Any railed enclosure is a wonderful spur to the imagination (see Chap. 7).

Fig. 8-12 The Gazebo. *(Courtesy Glassart Studio)*

*The Gazebo*

A larger sort of cage is shown in Figure 8-12. This one is gilded with stained glass all around and heavy wooden posts support it. There are four openings between the four major panels and there is plenty of room to walk through and admire the shifting colors. In addition to the spaciousness within, the effect of stained glass all around is an almost total luminescence of air; above, the double layers light up the sky, shifting as you move.

The gazebo is not complicated to build. As you can see, each major panel is broken into three vertical ones and three horizontal ones which form the roof. The major posts are two by fours. You don't even have to worry about anchoring it into the ground because its own weight will support it. So, if you've been won-

Fig. 8-13 The Easter Egg. (*Courtesy Rik Heidloff, photo by Rick Pawelka*)

dering what to do with that flat area of ground outside your porch, here's the answer.

*The Egg*

The Easter Bunny may not be able to carry this egg shown in Figure 8-13, but it can be an interesting novelty. The shape is made over a Styrofoam form in typical Tiffany fashion using copper foil. Glass globs are added over the surface to give it an ornate, regal appearance.

Mid-center you can place a small, hinged doorway that opens inward; this is one version of a "see through" Easter egg. Another method is to effect a line of cleavage approximately halfway across the surface so the top portion lifts off; this can be a good place to store colored Easter eggs. The globs can be arranged to run over the cleavage line so the egg opening will be hidden. This type of enclosure technique has multiple uses; this is one of its more sophisticated forms.

*The Fence*

No discussion of enclosure techniques would be complete without mentioning the fence—not an entire fence of stained glass but alternate or occasional sections of stained glass among the standard split rail or palisade wood sections. If you have a piece of property large enough to be fenced, this idea may prove colorful, distinctive and also use up a lot of those stained glass windows you can get inexpensively from your local antique shop,

Fig. 8-14 The Merry-Go-Round.

113

providing you're willing to spend some time doing repairs! We once acquired a number of windows in this fashion and many of them found their way, in time, to various fences in the area. Size doesn't matter; you can always fill in spaces around small windows with wood. If you can't find old windows, you can make your own; however, it's more fun to put the ancient tattered ones back into respectable use. They'll even outlast the wooden parts of the fence.

*The Merry-Go-Round*

Figure 8-14 shows an example of an enclosure that moves. It has a turntable motor, some plastic animals and heavy wire struts. The whole is enclosed in stained glass of a very simple design. The project is effective because it moves and because it provides a three-dimensional view of something within something else. This perspective always adds complexity even where there is none in the design.

# Chapter 9

# MIRROR, MIRROR . . .

A fascinating supplement to stained glass is mirrored glass. Mirror is easy to cut, readily foiled or leaded and can be used in slivers or large pieces, presenting an effect in whole or part that truly reflects the imagination of the worker.

## WORKING WITH MIRROR

Because of its particular fabrication, mirrored glass poses a few unique problems. Mirror is scored on its reflective surface, not its back. It should be cut like any other glass and broken out the same way, but care must be taken when cutting mirror so as to avoid even the minutest scratch on its back surface. Should such a scratch appear, it will probably show through the front and ruin the piece. Tapping the back roughly can also scratch it.

Another element that is rough on mirror backing is flux. Any flux, if left on the silvered portion of the mirror, will in time begin to dissipate it. This process generally starts at the border where the leading or foiling has taken place. Even if it doesn't spread much beyond this area, your final product will have an edge of moth holes around its mirrored portions. The obvious precaution is to wipe all flux off the mirror as soon as possible; even so, residues of the soldering process can weep from the surface for a long time. There is a mastic (a pasty material used as a protective coating) available from many commercial glass shops that will plug up these holes and scratches and if you find this happening once in a while to your mirrored pieces you might try it.

However, trouble with the silvered backing shouldn't be a constant thing. If it is, you may be using the wrong flux (oleic acid is still the best for mirror) and you may be scratching this surface while cutting. The mirror you purchased may have a special backing that just isn't amenable to stained glass use. One way to avoid this sort of problem is to thoroughly clean the back surface of any mirrored piece. Wait a day or two and rub it again. That won't put you through the looking glass, but it won't let your flux go through it either.

THE STAINED GLASS MIRROR

Probably the most logical way to use mirrored glass is to make a mirror out of it. Its borders are complemented with stained glass. First, an art nouveau design was selected and drawn on graph paper (see Fig. 9-1). Four rondels were chosen to help the swirling lines of this decor and in Figure 9-1 we can see the pieces of glass cut and placed on the graph paper to check for proper measurements.

Either of two methods may be used to place the central mirror. Either cut the mirror to fit between the irregular borders so that the finished product will be a flat plane or place it beneath the frame so that the end result will have a raised border of stained glass. To this latter choice, add the effect of reflection of the stained glass within the mirror. This gives an impression of even more depth than the raised surface alone can provide and is one of the bonuses of using mirror. For purposes of this display, we made the mirror fit between the stained glass pieces, while also traveling below what was to be a fairly complicated edging.

In Figure 9-2, we see how the stained glass border appeared after the pieces had been foiled and soldered together to achieve

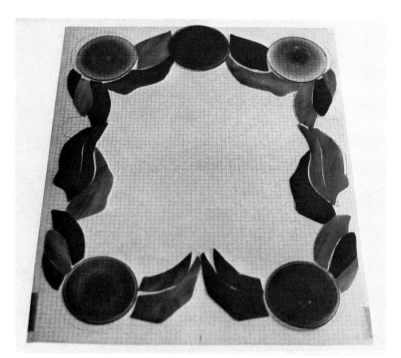

Fig. 9-1 Assembling the mirror border on graph paper to check evenness of design.

116

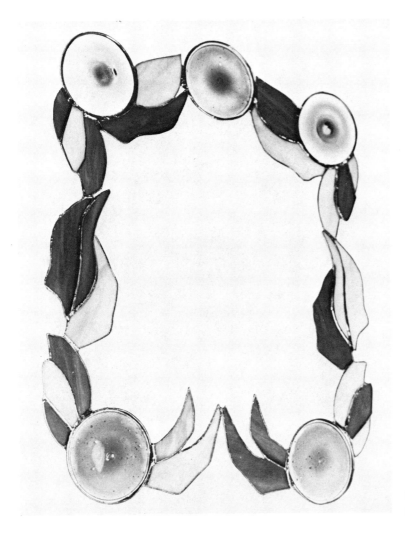

Fig. 9-2  The mirror border assembled and leaded.

the flowing effect typical of art nouveau. The mirror edge is also foiled, and the pieces of glass soldered to it. This is a shortcut of the usual process of putting together a panel whereby we would apply the top border of glass to the matching mirror edge and then the sides and bottom. However, when using one large piece of glass of any sort in the center of a bordering edge, you can get away with first doing the border and fitting the central portion to match afterwards.

Figure 9-3 shows the mirrored portion going into its central location. You can see at the bottom how the areas approximating the rondels are cut out to allow for a meeting of the mirror and rondel edges. Between the bottom rondels, however, the mirror has been left in one piece, permitting the stained glass in this area to flow upwards and over the lower mirror edge. We left the upper left corner slightly askew to show how this portion will tuck below that area of glass. Since this is opalescent glass,

117

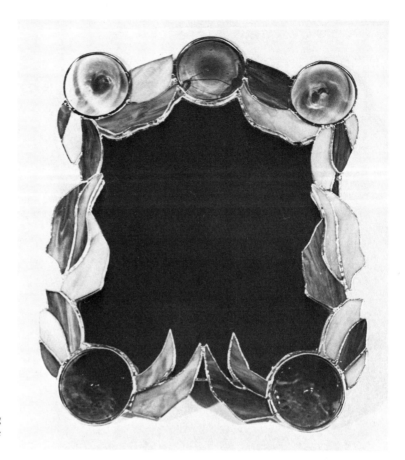

Fig. 9-3 The mirror being placed within its border. (See color section)

the mirror, where it does go under the glass will not show through. We do not care if small portions of the mirror show through the small spaces left between the upper glass pieces; we want the reflective effect here. This entire project is foiled and hangs cheerfully against any wall.

MIRRORED SHADES

This effect can be a garish one if not handled properly; it involves the use of mirror in lamp panels. Figure 9-5 shows a set made for a bedroom which combines a mirror framed with opalescent glass and a lampshade with alternating panels of mirror. We had to cover the mirrored panels with white paper for purposes of taking the photograph; the panels that show dark are green opalescent glass. The mirrored side faces outward on the panels. A lot of splashing of light occurs with this arrangement and, if the design of the lamp is too ornate, the addition of the mirror can be disasterous. Here, as you see, we purposely kept everything to a plain format.

118

Fig. 9-4 Another example of a stained glass bordered mirror—this one with an elaborate owl design. *(Photo taken courtesy of Hariette and Alden Getz)*

Fig. 9-5 Mirrored lamp panels and a matching stained glass mirror.

MIRROR AS A DESIGN ELEMENT

In these instances, the mirror is used for its sheen rather than for the practical purpose of reflection. It becomes the unusual central core of such a design, as shown in Figure 9-6 the basic decorative elements belong to the glass. Here the pieces fit compactly into the rondel shape. The addition of a painted design over the glass helps balance the dramatic flashing of the mirror.

Speaking of painting, you can print, stencil or paint on mirror as well as on glass. This technique can be provocative or annoying, depending on what you are using the mirror for. If function is mainly desired, such surface scribblings will get in the way. Crackled mirror—mirror that is purposely distressed and the pieces then glued together—will not be appreciated by someone who wants primarily a looking glass, and only as a last resort an objet d'art. Such techniques should be used only to bolster a design. As ends in themselves, they become tiresome.

MIRROR AS A PANEL

The above process of using a mirrored portion within a glass panel can be reversed to use glass within a mirror panel. Figure 9-7 shows one method of doing this. The border is opalescent glass and the central portion of mirror comprises the entire back-

Fig. 9-6 Decorative panel including mirror as part of the design.

120

Fig. 9-7 Mirror with inlaid stained glass.

ground. This is given break lines in the shape of a rose with two leaves. Opalescent glass is used for the figuration and it's important that it doesn't take up more than about one-third of the mirror surface—that way the reflective element is still functional. The novelty lies in exactly this characteristic and such mirrors, with inlaid stained glass designs of greater or lesser complexity, are unique objects to offer to a gift shop or make for friends who shouldn't only study themselves when they look in a glass.

MIRROR IN PIECES

Small pieces of mirror can also work with stained glass. In free form designs, they can be used as scales for fish, for sparkling or reflective elements within otherwise dark surfaces or for the tops or sides of boxes as glistening background. Their reflective element is useful to provide layerings of design even when the mirrored surface has been cut up in a Tiffany foil process.

# Part 2

# PROJECTS

*". . . the deliberately arranged climax
to which the whole construction
has been leading."*
Whall

# Chapter 10

# THE BIRDHOUSE

A project not strictly for the birds but one that could have a bit to do with feathering *your* nest is the birdhouse. Many people feed outside birds; witness the amount of wild bird seed and suet that is sold. And witness the number of birdhouses that are sold as well. None of these are cheep. A stained glass birdhouse might well become a status symbol; certainly it adds as much color and novelty to a backyard as the birds themselves. We have sold a number of them and even if you make them solely for your own use you'll not only please your eye but the birds as well. They really go for them.

## THE BASIC STRUCTURE

The basic structure is a box with a roof. All sides except the front and the bottom are made of glass. For supportive functions, the bottom is made of wood and the front is also wood for a very practical reason. We have found the bird can find his way through the doorway much easier if he is not distracted by a shiny glass facade. It also seems to be true that the wood does not get as cold as glass during the winter and we feel the house is therefore a little warmer. It is also easier to cut the doorway out of wood; if it were glass, we would have to make two halves, cut a semicircle out of each side and then foil the two halves together. Using wood we get a neater front view.

The sides of our birdhouse measure 9″ wide by 6″ high. Front and back are 8″ wide and 10″ high at the peak. The roof measures 9″ by 13″ wide, overlapping the front and back by 2″ and the sides by 2″.

## CUTTING THE PIECES

Patterns are made and the pieces are cut as usual except that the front piece will be cut out of sanded, thin plywood or pressed

Fig. 10-1 The birdhouse roof and the body: at top left, side pieces; at bottom left, front and back; at right, two roof pieces.

wood no more than ⅛″ thick (see Fig. 10-1). It is imperative that the measurements of the front piece match exactly those of the back piece or the house will be askew. We have had students who somehow felt because they were working with wood they could afford to get sloppy. This wood is going to be foiled in the same manner as the back piece of glass and the same dimensions must prevail. Cut all pieces before attempting to foil them into shape.

As for the type of glass to use, we prefer a transparent glass—an antique if possible, so that we can see through it and watch the birds within the house. One of the great disadvantages of wooden birdhouses is that you can't observe the birds inside. Since you are putting their food out at least partially to enjoy their company, a glass house will provide this if you use the proper glass.

If you really don't care about watching the birds inside the house, you can use opalescent. It's true this opaque glass creates more of an effect outside than does the antique or cathedral. The changing light swirls round it and it does not "black out" the way the transparent glass does when you look through two layers of it. So whatever glass you choose depends on what you expect from it; all we want to point out is that you should have an idea before you choose. And you should point this out to any potential customers as well.

*The Floor*

We generally cut this piece first. Square it up as perfectly as possible and cut it as fine as you can. All the other pieces will

126

take hold from this piece; and since it is to be immediately nailed onto a post to be set in the ground when the house is finished, it will be a little difficult to get it loose if you change your mind about a measurement. This is especially true once the glass portions are attached. Any pounding on the floor at that point will shatter them.

*The Doorway*

The doorway in the front section can be cut either before or after the edges are foiled. The area to be cut away is marked first by finding the center across the section and then by drawing a circle round it. A cutter for doorknobs works quite well for this. Measure out the proper size and place it in your electric drill (see Fig. 10-2). As in almost any drilling operation, the piece to be drilled should be held fast to a table to prevent it from rotating with the drill. This could be highly dangerous.

Once the circle is cut, you have your choice whether or not to foil it (see Fig. 10-3). Foiling does make it look neater.

Fig. 10-2 Opening the doorway. A doorknob drill is used.

Fig. 10-3 The front door with the doorway cut. Fiber board was used.

ASSEMBLY

When you have all the pieces ready to go, fabrication is quite simple. In fact you can do quite a number of these birdhouses at once—which makes it profitable if a number of your neighbors want one. The parts are matched together and soldered and once the basic framework is completed the roof can be angled into position (see Fig. 10-4).

Holding the back of the roof with one hand at the proper angle, tack the front portion and then reverse the procedure. With the roof stiffly soldered all along the seam, you are ready to fix it to the house. There are several ways of doing this. The easiest is to run wire from the inside peak of the house to the outside peak of the roof, front and back. While this will provide some stability, a good wind nosing under the eaves can rip the roof off all the same. The obvious answer would be to run a bead of Duco cement over the edges of the house and glue the roof into position. Unfortunately, you will have to clean your birdhouse eventually and the only logical way to do so is to take the roof off. This is difficult if you have cemented it to the house.

128

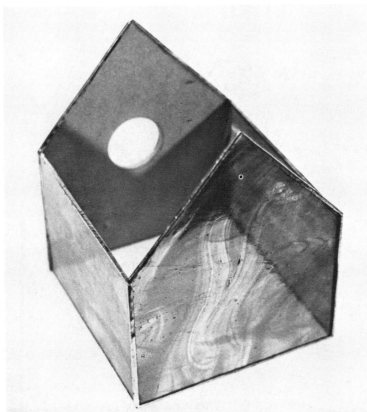

Fig. 10-4 Two side walls are foiled to the front and back.

Fig. 10-5 Ready for the roof.

Fig. 10-6 The Birdhouse project completed. The first tenant inspects it. (See color section)

We therefore use a wide band of filigree across the front and back near the peak which serves two purposes (see Fig. 10-5). It is decorative and makes a fancy perch for birds waiting their turn to get into the house and it provides a stable strut against which you can employ stiff wires from the inside peak to keep the roof on. Twist these wires to small eyes soldered into the roof seam at the overhang. This filigree banding is 3″ wide and is cut to the angles of the sides of the roof and soldered securely. It works well.

FINISHING TOUCHES

It's a good idea not to leave your wooden front raw; it should be painted and it's probably easiest to do so before fabrication. Generally we paint ours the same color as the glass we are using; but sometimes we use a totally different color. Painting adds finality to the project and helps the birds know that you really care.

If you wish, you can also electrify your birdhouse. A small bulb coming in from behind can dangle freely and at night will provide a striking illumination to your backyard, rather like a large stained glass lantern. Opalescent glass will probably show up best, but even the transparent glass will give your birds something to crow about.

130

# Chapter 11

# TOWNHOUSE TERRARIUM

Mountain greenery can be yours throughout your entire home if you utilize it within the bounds of a terrarium built to this shape. Stained glass terrariums have been enjoying an almost explosive popularity and there are more styles and varieties available than you can shake a jade plant at. We thought we would show how a simple effect can be accomplished utilizing mainly window glass so as to allow the maximum amount of light to get through, but emphasizing the notion by adding only three touches of stained glass in an ascending pattern. It's an interesting exercise in design.

## DESIGNING THE BASIC STRUCTURE

A difficulty in designing stained glass terrariums is the nature of the glass. To begin with, the color may not allow enough light to get through to keep the plants healthy. Most people don't make that mistake, however. The most common error is to use so much stained glass that the plant, which should be the central focus of attention, is overwhelmed. Other problems in design involve getting the plants in and out and maintaining the proper humidity. Too many terrariums start out being designed as lamps. There's a different kind of bulb that goes in a terrarium and the blueprint must be drawn with that in mind.

Our first presentation starts as a plain glass container with four sides and a bottom wrapped with copper foil and soldered tightly together. To give the sides more solidity and provide an evenness of border, we added four lengths of $3/16''$ U came over the foiled sides. The came is tacked top and bottom to the underlying foil (Fig. 11-1).

Next the top is added. These four pieces, also clear window glass, slant inwards at a very mild angle (see Fig. 11-2). Re-

Fig. 11-1  A very simple terrarium base.

member, we've got to be able to get plants in and out of the top and if this angle gets too great it will limit the amount of space available. It's a good idea to work these angles out first in cardboard. It will save a lot of frustration.

With the top pieces soldered into place—and the top can be put on in single pieces or as a unit—a lead "belt" is made by flattening a length of $^3/_{16}''$ came. This is now soldered around the juncture of top and bottom of the terrarium to hide the join and give a slightly decorative aspect to these otherwise plain walls. As a terrarium, the piece is finished; as a design, it is rather bland.

DESIGNING THE TOWNHOUSE

Figure 11-3 shows the completed townhouse into which the basic terrarium structure was converted. At the lower left corner a small planter extends out from the front wall. A red flemish glass in front, gives it a brick effect; the sides and bottom are flashed white opal glass which gives a pleasant effect against the red front. The little planter is tightly soldered outside and inside so it won't leak. Add some dirt and a few seeds and before you know it you'll have a plant growing out of it.

The off balance effect provided by the planter is compensated for by the door and the window. Although the window is glued into position we decided to foil its edges to give it a little more sparkle. If you decide not to foil this piece, make sure all edges are evenly cut and smoothly sanded; otherwise it becomes a great piece to cut your fingers on. Don't try soldering the window to the upper house rim; it doesn't look good there. We used a quick drying clear glue (Duco cement works well); take care not to use so much glue that it runs from behind down the surface of glass below. You can make a square window if you like; we preferred the curved top.

Fig. 11-2 A four-piece top is soldered onto the base at a slight angle.

133

Fig. 11-3 The complete
Townhouse Terrarium. (See
color section)

The door is also foiled both for design and for a practical effect. The right hand side of the planter is soldered into this rim
and the door is not only soldered along its foot into the bottom
edge of the terrarium, but is also glued along its back directly to
the front wall. We don't want it being torn off its hinges by the
weight of the planter.

And that's all the stained glass you need for this particular
project. You can get somewhat more ornate, if you wish, by adding a few windows on the other walls but we don't feel these do
anything and they tend to look just stuck on. Interestingly, the
terrarium still looks pretty bare without any plants. But it should.
If your terrarium appears completely finished without the plant,
you've over-designed the structure. With the plant in position

134

(we chose a fairly tall plant in a broad base for dramatic effect), the piece should look balanced and fulfilled.

ALTERNATE DESIGNS

Figure 11-4 shows a paper mock-up of a terrarium to be. It has not yet been decided whether the top will be removable or if a wide doorway will be cut in the front to allow entrance and exit. It's a good idea to carefully plan out your terrarium. These objects require more hours of labor than you might think, judging from their deceptively simplistic outline; and as in any three dimensional project, problems occur in depth. It takes a little longer to provide yourself with a mock up, but you'll save yourself time and material at the other end.

Fig. 11-4 Paper mock-up of a terrarium design.

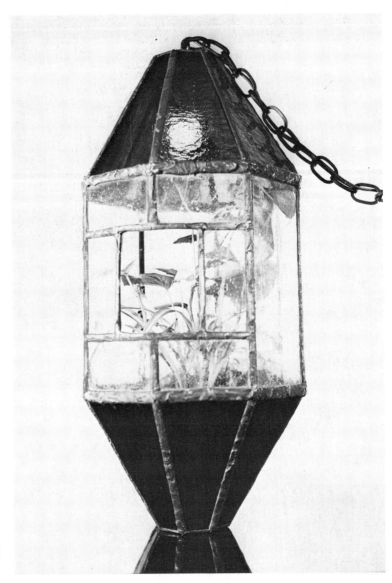

Fig. 11-5 Hanging terrarium with opalescent top and bottom.

Figures 11-5 and 11-6 show two other terrarium designs. Figure 11-5 demonstrates a hanging container with opalescent top and bottom but a clear center similar to the mockup in Figure 11-4. An open doorway leads to the small plant within. Such a doorway could also be hinged closed with an additional clear piece of glass if necessary to maintain proper humidity. Enough light is able to get through this amount of clear glass.

Figure 11-6 is an example of a removable top terrarium. This is a very ornate piece for a planter: it doubles as a lamp. The bulb inside provides the light for a number of small plants. With the top removed, the planter assumes a squat shape which is not

Fig. 11-6  A terrarium with
a removable top. This de-
sign doubles as a lamp.

unpleasant. The terrarium can be utilized in that form as well.
The outside filigree is all done by curling lead came which has
been first stretched absolutely flat not only to remove all kinks
but to prevent others from forming as the design is being fabricated.

137

# 12 Chapter

# THE SAILBOAT

This ship combines the use of sculpture, without actually bending the glass itself, and with copper wire as an integral part of the design.

THE PATTERN

Figures 12-1 and 12-2 provide the number and size of pieces needed for this project. You can vary your color choice a bit on the front sail (spinnaker) but other hues should be moderate since it is the front sail that is most spectacular. This project will help give you a sense of spatial arrangement that will come in handy when you begin to fabricate the Glass Galleon, the final project in the book.

All pieces should be cut to same size as those given in Figures 12-1 and 12-2 or increased proportionately if you want a larger boat. It is suggested that you cut all the glass for all sections before you start putting any of it together. Pieces 1, 3, 5, 7, and 9 must be cut twice; once as shown and once in reverse by turning the pieces of pattern over. The first group will attach to the left borders of pieces 2, 4, 6, 8, and 10; the second group to the right borders of those pieces. The remainder of the pattern pieces present little difficulty in cutting, especially if you employ special running pliers to get the edges as straight as possible. Pattern 11 will be the mainsail.

Figure 12-2 contains the patterns for the boat proper. Numbers 16 and 17 are the bottom of the hull; 18 and 19 form the sides; 20 and 21 form the prow; and 22 forms the back. You can see that numbers 16 and 17 form the actual shape of the boat; the other pieces taking their cue from the manner in which these pieces lie. Numbers 12, 13, 14 and 15 give a view of the boat from the top.

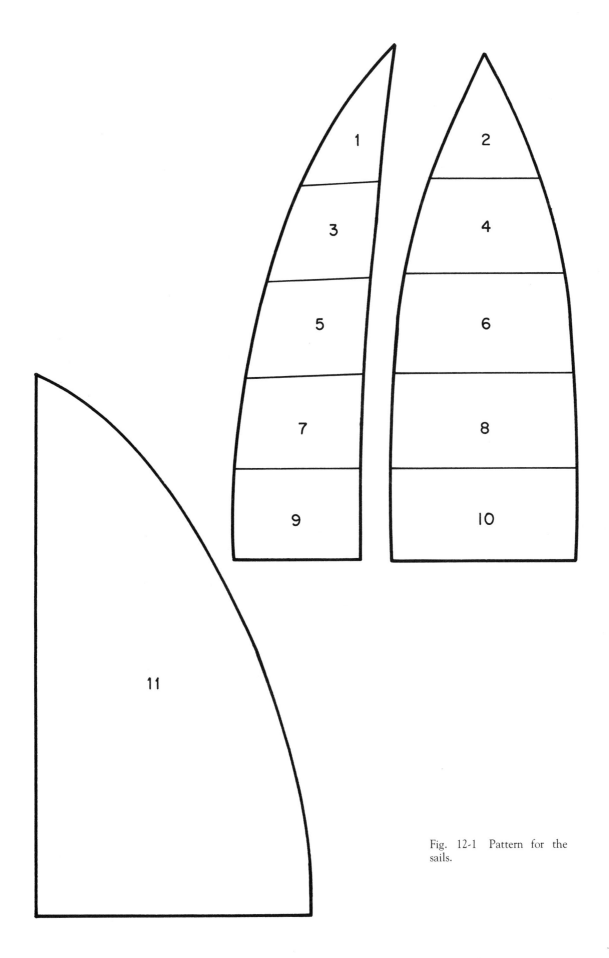

Fig. 12-1 Pattern for the sails.

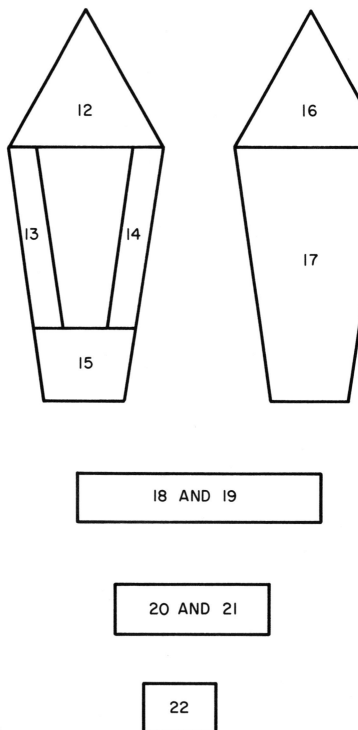

Fig. 12-2 Pattern for the boat.

*The Front Sail*

We are going to make a curved sail, using small straight pieces of glass. No mold is necessary since we can curve it pretty much to please ourselves. We do want the angles on either side to be even, but the final curvature depends on how the wind grabs us.

Figure 12-3 shows how this front sail is put together. There are five rows of three pieces, forming a triangle with the apex upward. Each piece is copper foiled and we have begun to tack the pieces together at the bottom. It is easy at this stage to bend these joints to the angle we want them—evenly on both sides. To get an idea how the outer line of the sail will look with this curve, we tacked into position the upper right top piece. Three pieces now remain to be fitted. Make certain the angle of the sail is how you want it and then go ahead and solder all the seams firmly.

Our color choice for this portion (all antique glass to give as gossamer a quality as possible) was as follows: bottom line orange, then red, amber, green and purple. You can't do that well with a real sail!

*The Main Sail*

Rather than cut out a lot of little pieces here, we decided to utilize a break-flow with copper wire (see Figs. 12-4 and 12-5). Five strands of this material are streamed along the width of the sail at intervals from the top. Angle them slightly. Soldering occurs to either border. You can tin the copper wire or not as you choose. These are the guy ropes. Not shown in Figure 12-4 is the wire that also crosses the back side of the sail. Although we used opalescent glass here, it is nonetheless imperative that you get

Fig. 12-3 The large front sail (spinnaker) being assembled in glass.

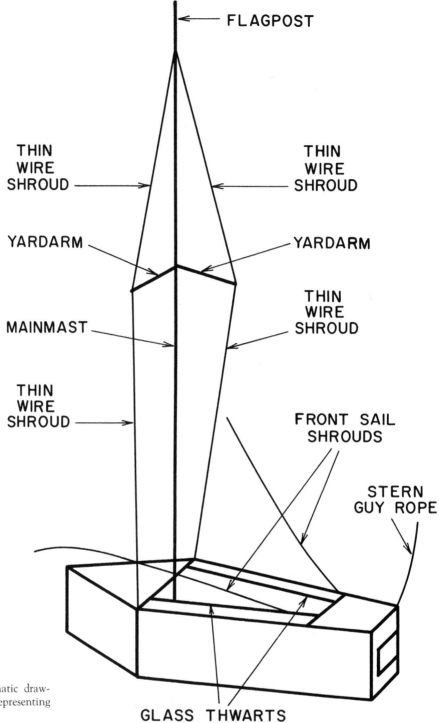

FLAGPOST

THIN
WIRE
SHROUD

THIN
WIRE
SHROUD

YARDARM

YARDARM

THIN
WIRE
SHROUD

MAINMAST

THIN
WIRE
SHROUD

FRONT SAIL
SHROUDS

STERN
GUY ROPE

GLASS THWARTS

Fig. 12-4   Schematic drawing of the wires representing lines.

142

Fig. 12-5 The completed project. (See color section)

the wire to lie evenly on both sides. When the sail is held up to the light, you don't want to see the shadow of the wire behind at a different level or angle to the one in front.

### The Boat

The small pieces of glass used for the boat should be all one color. We used a transparent brown as a neutral shade so as not to detract from the sails and to point up the overall design. Use of a single, transparent color throughout a three-dimensional object is interesting because the color varies in intensity, depending on whether it's being viewed in overlay or as a single plane.

If you were to look down on our glass boat, you would see that the center portion of the bottom, #17, is a lighter tone than the rest of the glass because the rest is seen in duplicate layers. The same effect occurs from the side, depending on the angle of sight.

Because the pieces of glass comprising this part of the project are small, we wrapped them in $3/16''$ foil. Assemble them from the bottom up starting with #16 and #17. Pieces #18 and #19 should go on top of #17, not alongside the borders; and #20 and #21 will follow suit with #16. Then solder #12 and #15 into position; follow that with the two side pieces #13 and #14 and you're ready, if not to sail, at least to float along.

### The Sails and Rigging

Cut yourself a copper wire mainmast $7\frac{1}{4}''$ long for a boat measuring $4''$ from bow to stern. On this basis, your front sail should measure $6''$ in height, including the curve and $5''$ at the base. There are no requisite dimensions but proportionately these match up pretty well. Your mainmast is to be a straight, heavy piece of copper wire and it should be tinned. The tinning process allows the mainsail to be soldered to it easily. Attach the base of the mast to the center of the bottom joint between #16 and #17 and also to the edge of #12 as it passes by. Use plenty of solder.

Next attach the mainsail to the mast. There should be $\frac{1}{2}''$ or so of mast on top and the bottom of the sail should clear the top of the boat by another $\frac{1}{2}''$. The mainsail is angled away from the perpendicular of the boat by $45°$.

Solder in place the stern guy rope—wire stretching from the tip of the back of the mainsail (back sail) to a point along the back wall of the boat. This also helps support the sail. Now cut the yardarm—a piece of wire about $1\frac{1}{2}''$ long which is soldered crosswise to the mast at a point $3''$ down from the top. Solder another wire to the right of the mast, the top at the level of the sail. Run it to the end of the yardarm; solder it there; then continue it down to the outside joint between #12 and #14 (Fig.

13-1). Solder it here as well. Repeat this with another wire to the left of the mast (see Fig. 12-4).

You are now ready to place the front sail (foresail). Attach its apex to the front of the mast a little below the juncture of the top of the mainsail. If you solder this firmly, the entire sail will be supported temporarily by this joint alone. Next measure the distances between the far ends of the front sail and the inner juncture line between #13 and #15 and #14 and #15. Cut two pieces of wire to these measurements and solder them in place as shrouds.

Clean the piece in the usual fashion and you've got a sturdy-looking, three-dimensional sailboat.

# 13 Chapter

# THE
# TRIPLE GLAZED
# BIRD

Gourmets think of a glazed bird as one glistening with syrup, fresh from the oven; we want to show you one made of stained glass that's even more digestible. Double glazing in glass craft implies the application of one piece of glass directly over another. This can be especially tricky with stained glass since, if you are not careful, one tone may cancel out the other, leaving you with a colorless result. The object of multiple glazing is to achieve texture and emphasis; if the technique is used within a panel, as Tiffany often did, a stark angulation is created between background and foreground that hustles the eye. The technique is equally effective on its own; as a measure of its commitment to figuration, we want to show you how to triple glaze a small-pieced free-form ornament.

THE BASIC DESIGN

Since our idea was to present a robust object in a strong geometric pattern, made even more assertive by use of this triple-glaze technique, we settled on the triangle. To our mind, the triangle is the most forceful geometric pattern; we have often used it as such in designing windows. For texture we chose feathers; a feathered triangle reminded us of a seated bird and we decided to use a series of overlapping triangles to present the multiple glazing. However, it was only the feathers we wanted in stained glass layers; otherwise the body of the bird would become a hodge-podge of colors. We used stained glass for the body only at the end. For the first and intermediate layers, the body is window glass.

Another emphatic portion of the bird was to be its beak and eye. This, up top, would balance the force of feathers below. Accordingly, we designed the body as basically triangular with an indication of where the beak would go and with an irregular line at the base where the feathers would protrude (see Fig. 13-1). Since we decided on an overall measurement of no more than 10″, we split our layers of glass to about 7″, 8½″ and 10″ in length. The width would measure 6″ across the lowest feathered area and 4″ at the top of the head.

## USING WINDOW GLASS

Just because you're working with window glass is no reason to cut carelessly. Since you are going to be cutting this one pattern four times and each pattern must fit exactly atop the other, it behooves the worker to make precise cuts. There's no room for grozing into the basic shape to make up for errors in cutting.

At first the basic shape doesn't look like much (see Fig. 13-1). Nevertheless, smooth the edges and foil the piece. Above all, keep it clean. This is going to be the most repetitive part of the whole project. You must continually rub fingerprints and flux

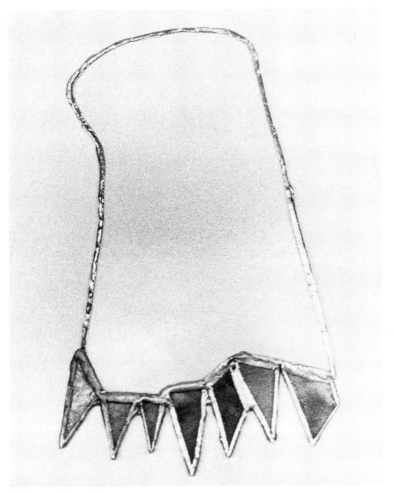

Fig. 13-1 The basic triangular shape in window glass and the first set of feathers along the irregular bottom surface.

residues off the glass. The longer you let them remain, the harder they will be to remove and the more likely they will be sandwiched between the layers. As you finish each layer, clean the glass thoroughly and handle it only by the edges. Then solder it to the next clean piece. Don't flux the edges much when soldering the layers together; flux will run between the layers and cloud the glass.

FEATHERING THE GLASS

There will be three separate layers of window glass with feathers attached, one front layer of stained glass without feathers and one back layer of flashed white opal without feathers. In Figure 13-1, we see the first layer being formed. All the feathers are foiled and run along the irregular length of the base. Despite the fact that they are going to partially rest on other pieces of glass, you should solder all pieces front and back. No beading here—just flat soldering.

In Figure 13-2, you can see how the first two layers are going to go together. Here the two window glass overlays are hinged with solder at the head to demonstrate how closely they are aligned. As you progress along the feathered scale to the next layer, the space left for feathers above will be less, filled in by the previous two layers, and the spaces for the lower feathers will automatically present themselves. No feather should directly overlay another except along its border. There's plenty of room here dimensionally and the whole idea is to have layers of *integral* feathers, providing an illusion of great depth as the light comes through. You can see this idea demonstrated in Figure 13-2. Imagine the top level has been put in place on the lower; the

Fig. 13-2  The first layer attached to the second layer. The body shape is the same but feather placement varies so as to fall between those above.

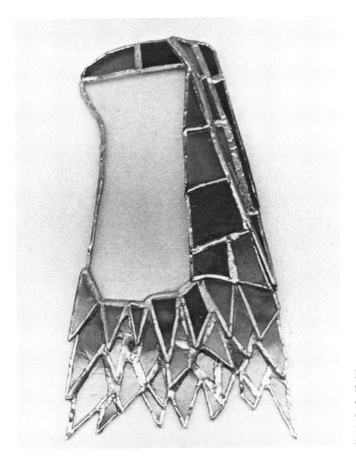

Fig. 13-3 Three layers of feathers, one below the other, are completed. None overlap. The body shape is now receiving its coating of stained glass pieces.

spaces above the feathers on the lower level will be filled by the feathers of the upper level. The next piece of feathered glass will do the same for the spaces below feathers on the second level. This is seen clearly in Figure 13-3 where the feathered layers have been completed and the body of the bird is being assembled.

BUILDING THE BODY

The feathers, of course, are triangular; and carrying this geometric motif to its conclusion, the elemental design within the body is triangular. You can see the beginning of this in Figure 13-3 where the first two out of what will be the four body triangles are in place. The glass is foiled and the pieces soldered together directly over the upper surface of window glass. The irregular surface of the base of the window glass is maintained to give a craggy appearance and a sharp dimensional feel. The two outer lines of the body that you see in place in this figure are slanted from base to head to further enhance this layered effect. To emphasize the triangulated push, we are going to separate these blocks by lead lines. Lead is used as exclamation points in

149

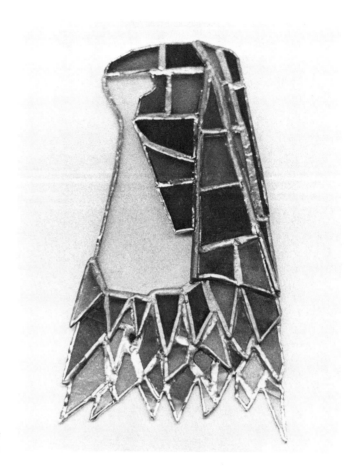

Fig. 13-4 The body shape
continues to be covered over.

the design. Here you can see the first large triangle containing
five pieces of foiled glass, the sides of which are snugged into lead
came. Figure 13-4 shows the next body triangle with its foiled
pieces fitting into the open channel of the lead came already
present.

Notice that although the pieces of glass seem to be going
in according to a pattern, there are no guidelines visible. Certainly we made no marks on the body; we'd never be able to get
them off. Our design was drawn on paper to exact dimension and
we cut the glass from that.

Now, in Figure 13-5, you can see the beginning formation of
the eye socket and the clustering of glass around the area of the
beak while another body triangle is being fitted. The lead came is
being helped into place with the leading knife; it's critical that
the foiled edges of glass fit properly within the channel. The extended lead to the right of the one triangle being worked on has
been left long to be the guideline for the beak. It will be cut right
at the boundary line of the body where the beak lead will meet it.
The came used here is ⅛″ H round; ³/₁₆″ can also be used
without overbalancing the design.

150

We have now completed the body of the bird. We used antique glass throughout without overlapping any pieces. Straight lines only have been employed to give the rugged feeling this object should produce. Colors are bright, lively ones: reds, oranges, greens, blues and yellows in varied shadings.

FORMING THE EYE AND THE BEAK

Figure 13-6 shows the eye in place. We used an orange half flat "jewel" 1″ in diameter; orange or red makes for a wicked looking eye. This is foiled and soldered to the borders of the surrounding glass pieces. The first portion of the upper beak is foiled in next to it.

This area calls for the only opalescent glass used in the project. We used a yellow opal for the top of the beak; black glass for the bottom section. In Figure 13-7 which shows the completed bird, you will note that the beak is composed of four sections. What you cannot see here is that we made the beak slightly tilted, adding depth by keeping the lower portion in the same plane as the body, but building the upper portion out over it on a slant. We used a wide ¹/₁₆″ U lead to do this, starting from below the beak to meet with the long body lead previously noted and up the top

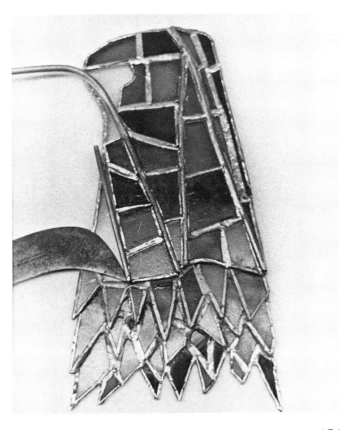

Fig. 13-5 Completing the stained glass body formation. Note the way lead came is being used.

151

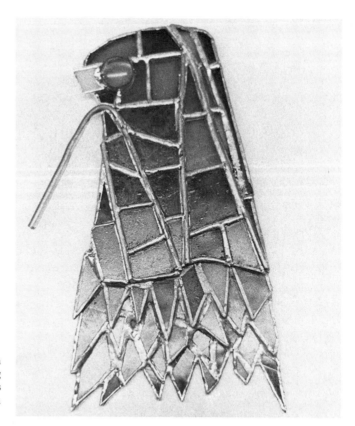

Fig. 13-6 The eye is in place and the beak is being formed. All stained glass body sections are placed in position now.

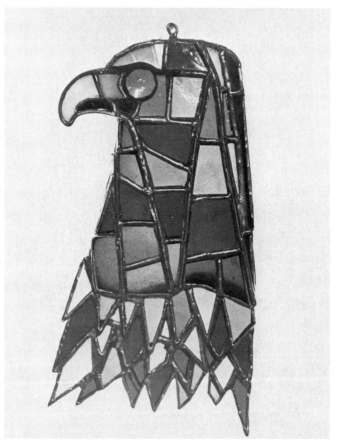

Fig. 13-7 The completed Triple Glazed Bird project. Note how the beak is emphasized by lead lines around it and by jutting forward beyond the glass. (See color section)

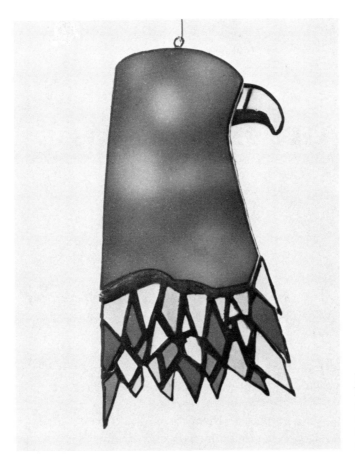

Fig. 13-8 The bird from behind with a piece of flashed
white opal glass to complete
the background. Note how
the light comes through in
mysterious patches.

side to continue directly over the glass edge of the body, over the
eye and about half-way back. This also forms the eyebrow.

With the placement of the beak, the design itself is con-
cluded. However, due to the special technique utilized, one
problem remains: the bird seen from behind does not give the effect desired. The eye is missing, the body foiling is less powerful
and the feathers are in the wrong perspective. In short, this is a
piece of stained glass that is meant to be viewed from one side
only. Here was a unique occurence: it meant we could not hang
the bird in a window; only against a wall. There it looked effective but hampered. We decided to give the bird a more specific
backing to go with the very specific forefront.

As you can see in Figure 13-8, a piece of flashed white opal
was cut to close in the piece and turned out to be exactly right for
the conception. This tells the viewer, first, that this area of the
bird is the back; it makes the front provocative by allowing hints
of colored light to filter through; and it provides a designed ending to a designed statement.

# 14 Chapter

## THE MENORAH

Glass and stone go together very well. Here's a project utilizing a special kind of rock together with chunk "rock-like" glass. Lava rock pieces, which can be acquired at most garden shops, are not cheap (they run about 50 cents a pound) but they are not heavy and yet give a massive effect and are readily worked. Their acquiescence in this regard is important; we have tried incorporating rocks of all types in designing sculptured pieces and most of them can frustrate an entire effort by chipping, flaking or crumbling at critical junctures. Lava is good natured; like balsa wood it responds to fingers.

WHERE TO BEGIN

The idea is to design a piece that is dramatic, forceful and at the same time delicate as a flame. For this we used chunk glass from dalles de verre or slab glass. Such chunks can be purchased by the pound in supply stores and, if you are fortunate, you may find pieces already pretty well shaped to your needs (see Fig. 14-1). All you are looking for are straight pieces of indeterminate length, depending on what size you want your project to be. Our menorah central column stands approximately 8″ high and contains seven glass chunks each roughly 1½″ long and 1¼″ wide. If you can't find chunks to these dimensions, you can lop off sections of larger pieces to requisite size. You don't need fancy tools for this, especially if this is a one-time project. However, you obviously aren't going to get very far attempting to cut chunks with a glass cutter. Using a standard table vise (which you will need for another part of this project anyway), position a chisel so that it is locked in place edge upward. Hold your chunk against this edge and hit from the top with a bricklayer's hammer—the closest you can get to a dalle hammer without spending all that money. A regular hammer may suffice but you run the risk of

154

Fig. 14-1 Chunk glass pieces typical of those used in this project.

shattering or, at least, chipping your top surface because of the excessive pressure. Your glass chunk should separate neatly, almost effortlessly, once you acquire the knack of how hard to hit. A sudden sharp tap is better than a wind-up pound.

Don't go overboard on colors here; you can use one color all the way through your chunks and either vary it or continue it in the arms or you can alternate two colors. The design is striking enough; too much color, more than two colors, will tend to blur its focus.

## MAKING THE CENTRAL COLUMN

With your chunks hewn to proper shape, put them together end to end with the flattest edges touching. You will have to work with two pieces at a time; do not attempt to fabricate the whole column at one fell swoop. Once you decide on the arrangement, glue the pieces together with Duco cement. Then wrap ¼″ or ⅜″ copper foil tape around the joints. The tape should overlap the joints by a good ¼″. Solder the foil all around. Repeat this process with the other chunks and allow the glue at least an hour to bind properly. Don't try to avoid using glue. You may feel that adhesive-backed tape is sufficient to hold your piece together, but it's probable in this instance your menorah will need a lot of prayers.

Now join the two-chunk pieces together in the same fashion, keeping the column as straight as possible. It doesn't matter which is the top or bottom end; it doesn't matter if the column bows slightly to right or left. We're after a primitive "rugged" look after all; not machine-made perfection. This should not, however, be an excuse for shoddy workmanship.

## FORMING THE ARMS

With the central column completed, you can turn your attention to the arms (see Fig. 14-4). They must be in proportion to the central column but need not be of the same type glass. (See the finished project in the color section for placement of arms.)

155

We feel using chunks for the arms overweighs the piece. It also detracts from the flames which will be chunk glass pieces. Our advice, therefore, is to use opalescent glass for the arms in a color complementary to one of the hues in the central column.

Calculate where the arms will be joined to the column; these must be soldered into place against the copper foil, holding the central chunks together. Our horizontal arms measure as follows: bottom 4″, next 3″, next 2″ and the top 1″. All measurements are taken to the joint with the vertical arm.

The arms should be leaded, not foiled; foiling would make them look too delicate. Use a $^1/_{16}$″ U came and fit it tightly to all surfaces. Once leaded, the arms are soldered to the column joints where they balance best. You can move them up or down the column as long as you leave enough lead-foil surfaces to solder against. They should be soldered midway across the width of the column; the tendency is to solder the piece flat against your work surface which will not center the arms and will unbalance the piece. Put a couple of thicknesses of cardboard under the arm you are soldering to bring it up from the table and more level with the middle of the central column.

For purposes of stability, the arms should be supported to each other. Do not affix them all together; this makes the flow of line monotonous. The two lower arms may be soldered together along the vertical sections and the two upper arms may be treated the same way. The gap between the two arm sections intrigues the eye and makes it see each arm as a discrete entity.

MAKING THE FLAMES

We turn to chunk glass once again for the flames because we are after a forceful, irregular pattern which would be diminished by using sheet glass. We want dimension here and plenty of it. We also want to do something a little different as far as the relationship of the flame to the candle is concerned. Simply wrapping the chunk flame with copper foil and soldering it to the underlying candle would indicate combustion but we want to see flame freely leaping off the wick. A foil wrapping would interfere with this; so would a juxtaposition designed to hold the pieces together.

We solved the problem by using wire. This allows us to use the flame chunks just as they are and to gap them off the candles. Thin copper wire is used; the thinner the better so the eye will take as little note of it as possible (see Fig. 14-4).

Each chunk flame is placed in a vise and a hole is drilled in its base with a ⅛″ glass drill (see Fig. 14-2). The hole should be at least ¼″ deep. The hole is then filled with Duco cement and the copper wire is inserted. In order to provide as much surface as pos-

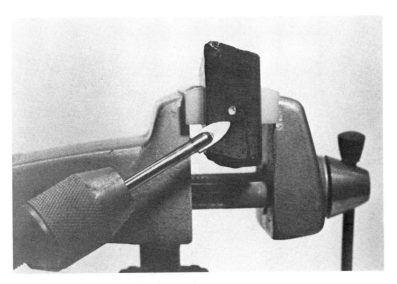

Fig. 14-2 Drilling a hole in a glass chunk.

sible for the glue to grab, the wire is looped within the hole (see Fig. 14-3). Enough wire is measured out to provide a reasonable gap between candle and flame as well as a solderable amount to be attached to the upright arm of the menorah.

Once the glue dries, the free end of the copper wire is right-angled and soldered to the underlying arm. We did not do this in the central section of the menorah, preferring to glue on a larger, more forceful flame as a sort of dividing line across the design. For purposes of demonstration, the central flame's effect may be

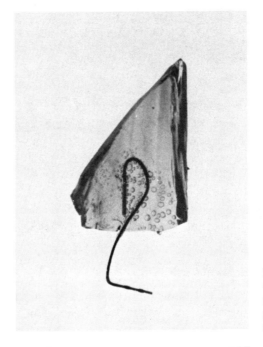

Fig. 14-3 Glass chunk piece with wire glued in hole. The free end of the wire will be glued to the end of the glass arm of the project.

157

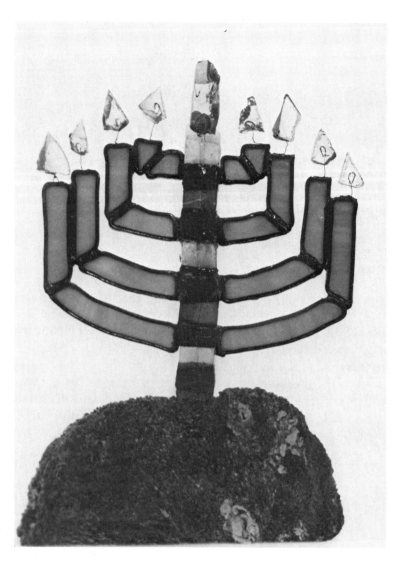

Fig. 14-4 Completed Menorah. (See color section)

calculated against the other wired flames and the reader may decide which provides more excitement to the design.

ATTACHING THE BASE

As stated above, we used a lava rock for the base. The granitic effect provides an upward sweep and complements the rugged nature of the piece itself. The rock stands 5" high and spreads 9" across—a substantial base. If it were smaller, the menorah would look silly perched atop it; more massive and the candleholder would be lost. Practically speaking, we also needed dimensional capabilities that would allow the menorah to stand upright without tipping; it is topheavy as you might imagine. We therefore chose our base with care, picking a rock that rose to a fairly abrupt crest and that had a flat under surface.

158

Once we decided, we chose a spot along the crest that looked interesting (not in the center but not extremely to either edge) and with an electric drill bored a hole into the rock. You can readily do this with lava and it's a lot safer than trying to chip it by hand with a chisel which will probably split the rock. Our hole was about 1½″ deep and somewhat more than the width of the menorah stem—roughly 1¼″. A good bit of crumbly rock and dust comes out of the lava when you drill; tap it out of the hole and carefully watch your depth. When we had gone to what we considered by measurement was the proper depth, we seated the menorah in the hole and, having previously heated beeswax in a pot, the same process employed in "waxing up" painted windows (see techniques on painting), we dropped small amounts of melted wax into the hole with a medicine dropper. It doesn't take long for the wax to begin to hold the stem. At this point, the stem can still be moved so if you aren't sure it is straight, use a level and make sure. Continue to drop wax into the hole with the dropper, going around the central column. You will feel the column being held more and more rigidly. Fill the hole right up to the top with the wax; the porous nature of the stone makes a very strong bond with the beeswax and you needn't worry about the wax giving way. Once it is hard—a matter of a few moments only—you can move your menorah in any direction without fear of its coming loose.

As a finishing touch, you can glue a piece of felt to the bottom of the stone if you are afraid it might scratch your furniture.

# 15 Chapter

# THE
# SMILING
# MONK

Utilization of the silk screen technique will allow you to mass produce these friars faster than a Kentucky Colonel. Stained glass items need not always be broken with lead lines. Unique items can be processed artistically *and* rapidly. You can certainly paint your monk by hand; and if all you desire is one for your own pleasure, this would be the way to go about it. But if you've got a lot of friends—or, better still, customers—all of whom would like a smiling monk, you have to find a serviceable way of supplying them. Silk screening on glass is one answer.

## THE SILK SCREEN TECHNIQUE

Silk screening is really a method of printing, using a fine mesh to strain the desired image onto the requisite surface. Each of the multiple tiny holes in the silk acts as a disposer to keep the ink or paint within discrete spaces. These areas of separation are too small for the eye to make out but if they were not there blurred paint would be the result. The screen is at once a holding and a transfer medium and must be kept taut and wrinkle free.

The best way of doing this is to make a stiff frame for it; one that will accomplish not only the purpose of supporting the transfer, but one designed to do it as efficiently as possible. The equipment shown here in Figure 15-1 is the complete production line. It's simple and easily assembled yourself. Of course, if you don't want to make your own (and there are any number of books that tell you how to do so), you can purchase silk screen set-ups in most artist's supply stores. There are no modifications necessary for glass in the basic mechanics.

## THE DESIGN

In Figure 15-2, we show the gradual emergence of our monk from the sketch on the left to the more finely drawn and inked in

160

Fig. 15-1 The silk screen frame and stencil used for this project. Two additional plain pieces of stencil paper are shown.

central figure and then, on the right, the final product ready for stenciling. You can screen very complicated drawings if you wish but remember that you are dealing with glass, not cloth; you want the glass to be the imperative factor and the paint lines an attribute. We have arranged the design to take up the entire glass

Fig. 15-2 The basic drawing in three stages of development.

161

blank; the color of the glass, sparkling through, will give the figuration its identity. For your first project with screen printing, it's a good idea to stay simple; you will be the one to cut the stencil.

THE STENCIL

We like a paper stencil for silk screening glass; we find this gives nice crisp lines. You can use typing paper or buy stencil paper in an art supply store. Cut the stencil with a sharp knife. A stencil knife is better than a razor blade for this because it offers more mobility to the wrist and allows you to make a more perfect match between the painting you want and the design you get. Use thin paper; the thicker the paper, the harder it is to cut and if you have to go over a line that you've only partly cut chances are you will end up with a ragged border. There is also the possibility of ending up with too much ink on the glass if your paper stencil is thick. The heavier the paper stock, the more ink or paint you will push through the screen, the longer it takes to dry and the easier it is to smudge within the process.

Always draw the final design directly on the paper stencil and remember to keep it clean; otherwise it won't stick to the screen. The first passage of paint over the stencil should flatten it to the screen; from then on you pass your glass blanks under it to turn out a practically inexhaustible supply of monks.

This is not to suggest that we do not use other types of stencils besides paper. We like film and self-sticking stencils as well. We suggest that before trying this project, you get hold of a book on silk screening and master the techniques. It is a simple enough operation and very effective.

THE SQUEEGEE

The squeegee is the spreader; it is to silk screening what the paintbrush is to painting. This object, drawn over the screen and either pulling or pushing a bead of paint before it, delivers the message to the glass blank beneath. It is no more than a piece of tough, flexible rubber in a handle that can be gripped firmly. A wooden frame is best but plastic can be used if it is thick enough. It is important that the squeegee be wide enough to cover the entire design, so it can spread the paint with only one stroke.

THE BLANKS

In Figure 15-3, the two basic blanks used for this project are seen. The upper left is copper (or sheet metal if you prefer) and is the master pattern used to cut the paper patterns which in turn are used to cut the glass. When you make a great many glass shapes using the same paper pattern, the paper eventually wears

162

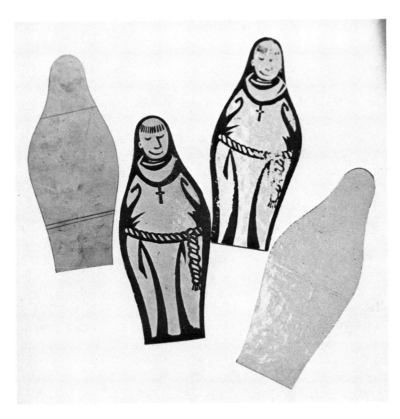

Fig. 15-3 Upper left, a metal blank; lower right, a glass one. Two stenciled figures are shown.

down and the shape begins to change ever so slightly. Long before this happens, you would be wise to make another paper pattern from the master.

Since this screening involves the entire surface of the glass blank, a discrepancy in the glass will throw the stenciled form awry. Metal blanks of thin sheet metal should be made very carefully to the exact size required and all borders should be smoothed with a file or a Carborundum sander. When tracing this blank onto pattern paper, use a thin, sharp pencil point and cut just on the pencil line. If you fail to do this, your resulting pattern will come out a trifle larger or smaller than the blank.

On the lower right in Figure 15-3, the glass blank itself is seen, duplicating exactly the metal one above. Before we do any screening, we cut fifty or sixty of these blanks so that when we set up to print we can whiz right along. The name of the game is efficiency.

Between the two blanks are two finished monks; one good, the other not so good. Neither of these has yet been fired so the painting is only temporary. The not-so-good monk has had some problems with the silk screen. The paint has not taken too well. There are several reasons why this may happen.

163

*The stencil was poorly cut.* Everyplace you wish to show paint on the glass blank must have an exit cut into the stencil so that paint can flow through the screen. Go over the stencil carefully before starting the painting to make sure this is done. Small areas such as the hairline in this monk can be easily overlooked or the holes can have ragged borders. The same is true of the face and the cassock rope. These are fine details and cannot be done hurriedly. Note the difference in these details in the monk on the left.

*The glass was not clean.* You should go over each glass blank as it is used with some sort of glass cleaner. Don't give these items a wipe with the palm of your hand; some of the oil from your skin will latch on to them and spoil the painting. The blanks should be perfectly dry when you use them. Paper towel is good for this purpose.

*Use the proper paint.* Squeegee® Black paint is what we generally use. This can be acquired from most dealers that supply glass artists. It is a paint specially made to be used with silk screening and applies well to the glass. It is a deep black and maintains its hue even when used thinly.

*Use the proper consistency.* The same problems apply to screening paint on glass as when using a brush; most of these have to do with the consistency of the paint. If it is too thin, it will barely stay on the glass; too thick and it may smudge or take forever to dry. The consistency keeps changing as the medium—water and vinegar—keeps evaporating. This is one of the reasons we advise having a large number of blanks on hand when you start to screen. The more paint you mix, the longer the consistency will be maintained. A lot of the paint will end up at the bottom of your screen with the downward stroke of the squeegee. If you have more of the proper consistency mixed, you can keep adding this amount to it and you will be able to work for some time.

*Avoid any movement of the glass.* Just as it takes practice to judge paint consistency, it takes some trial runs with the squeegee to find out how much pressure to apply. The commonest result of too much pressure is movement of the glass blank below the screen. You will get a result similar to the smudged cassock rope in Figure 15-3. Make sure that the blank is well supported. Old newspapers will do a good job; they are sturdy, wide and provide a certain amount of "give" that can compensate for overenthusiasm with the squeegee.

*Avoid mishandling the painted blank.* This is more common among individuals who are used to screening ink onto surfaces other than glass. Glass paint is not permanent until it is fired into the surface; if it is subjected to over-hearty embraces with

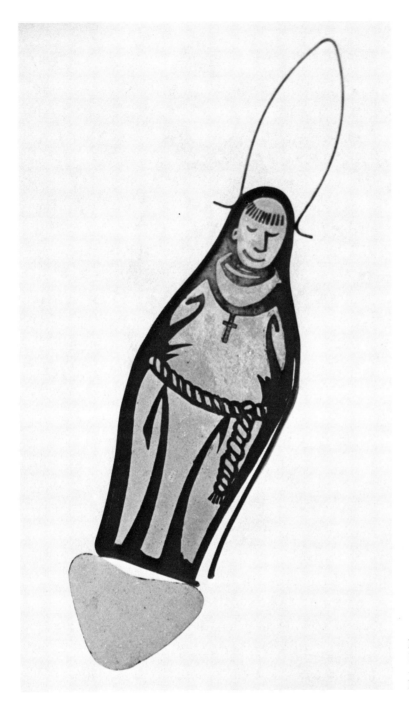

Fig. 15-4 The monk being
leaded, hanged and stood
—according to how you want
him.

the fingers, chances are that the paint so carefully screened on
will flake off. You can see the result of this sort of thing in the
outline of the monk on the right in Figure 15-3. The paint along
its left side is chipped. In such an instance, even if this is all that
is wrong with the result, the paint must be removed and the
screening redone.

Fig. 15-5   The finished product.

Once you have your monk painted and fired, lead him. We like to use $^1/_{16}''$ U lead and in Figure 15-4 we show the monk being leaded with a few alternative end results. The leading itself is simple enough—provided you press the came firmly into place especially at the dips of the neck and round the bottom angles. These are the areas from which it will fall away otherwise. There is only one joint to solder; make it halfway across the bottom if you are going to stand your monk. If you intend to hang him, make it one of the bottom angles. The joint is most unobtrusive at these areas.

The bottom plate should be made of the same glass as the

166

monk. It's not meant to stand out, just stand. To hang, the top clip is pressed together so the two points meet the ridge of border lead behind and they are soldered to it.

Figure 15-5 shows our finished product on a base. How much material was used? Two pieces of glass, half a strip of lead came, a small amount of paint and little labor.

# 16 Chapter

# COAT OF ARMS WINDOW

Let us postulate a commission to you as it was put to us. A gentleman named Torro wished to have a coat of arms made. It was to have an uncrowded look, was to fit into a lightbox (which would also have to be made; see Glossary) not larger than 2′ by 1½′, was to have some painted detail and was to indicate his Spanish ancestry and his wife's French ancestry.

THE DESIGN

*The Linear Quality*

The first step was to provide ourselves on paper with the exact amount of working space. Obviously this was not going to be a small-pieced Tiffany window. We envisioned a design of slashing lines against a central core which would carry the messages inherent in the commission. This central core would be divided at least in half for the French and Spanish sections; but probably in thirds to allow a central section for the actual design. For a start we drew a horizontal line across the space approximately two-thirds from the bottom. The straight linear quality was too divisional and we shortened the line so that it gapped away from the borders (see Fig. 16-1a).

Rather than divide the remaining space in half with a similar line, we worked the device against the line we already had. Coats of arms usually mean a shield and so we provided one using our top line as one edge (see Fig. 16-1b). We ran the point of the shield down to a position about two-thirds of the remaining space. We did not wish our divisional areas to appear too even. Basically we now had our space divided into thirds: the area atop the first line, the middle section of the shield and that area below the point of the shield. By a modified projection of the curve of the shield, we extended our top line to either border (see Fig. 16-1b).

Fig. 16-1a–f The formulation of the design of the Coat of Arms panel as discussed in the text.

Fig. 16-1b

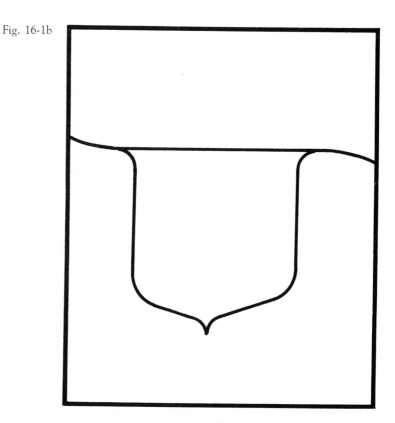

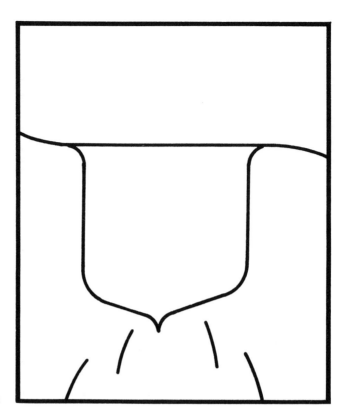

Fig. 16-1c

Fig. 16-1d

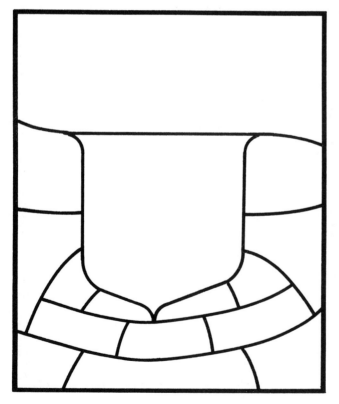

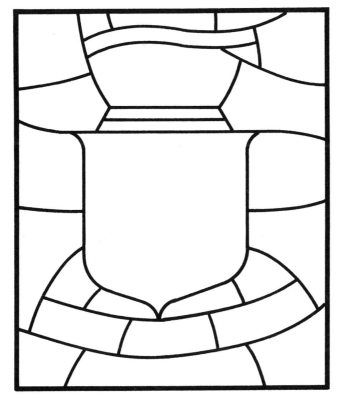

Fig. 16-1e

Fig. 16-1f

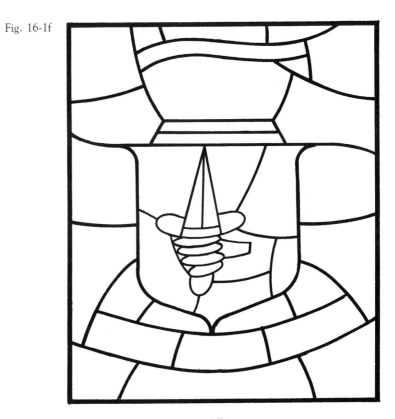

We now had to find a way to divide the lower space and at the same time attach the free-floating end of the shield to a design which could be cut out of glass. The obvious continuation of the point to the lower border via a straight line was meaningless and a dead end. We decided to add some lines mimicking the curve of the shield (see Fig. 16-1c). We already had expressed that curve and now we would echo it in miniature. We placed four lines, two attaching to the lower border and two indented into the remaining space, temporarily floating. Now we had increased our possibilities.

Looking at the design there now was one line that seemed perfectly logical: one that would cross from left to right borders and connect up with the tops of the two lower lines and the bottoms of the two upper ones. Accordingly we drew it in (see Fig. 16-1d). Our lower portion was now secure, but we still had the upper ends of those lines wagging in the breeze. We decided to duplicate the line we had just drawn and connect up the point of the shield with our two free ends. However when this line was completed, it looked too much like the first, so we withdrew the ends from the borders and provided a curved line to either side of the shield to meet it and terminate against the line below. This left us with two awkward spaces under the shield in the light of lines we had already drawn. We broke those up with lines complementing the bottom two curves. Now there was too much space to either side of the shield; we split these spaces with curves opposed to those immediately below. We had now carried this part of the design as far as we could for the present. Although the lines in the sketch in Figure 16-1d are equally accented, we had already determined which would be background lines and which foreground and we would emphasize this in the leading.

We had now to turn our attention to the top third of the design. This was to stand against and complement the bottom two-thirds. To isolate this section a little more, we added two more lines above the shield providing a sort of no-man's-land between the two top portions of the central core (see Fig. 16-1e). We did not wish to carry this isolation into the background of the design; so we abbreviated it with a curved line to either end, terminating in the top of the shield. From here two curved lines extended to the top border with the space between them to be taken up by another device.

We decided the panel was unbalanced. There was too much space on top against the linear degree of the bottom. It was also too balanced with the one large top space sitting above the large middle space, even with the extra lines between. We unbalanced the top space by breaking it irregularly with two major lines. The first cut it off from the top border, making it more interesting; the second, from the right side, gave the top space five sides instead of four—a different rhythm. The addition of some background lines to make the pieces more suitable for cutting gave us our rough sketch of what the basic design would be like (see Fig. 16-1e).

Figure 16-1f shows the middle space containing a hand holding a dagger with ten requisite breaks; the dagger would be painted and cut; the hand mostly painted. We also added another line in the top which took up some of the small space to the right. Our intention was to balance the lowest third; both these areas would contain lettering. The top line would contain the family name and below the name an emblem of some sort; since the family name was Torro and since animal devices are common in heraldry, why not a bull? Our thinking was now fairly complete though all we had on paper was the linear flow. Yet, starting with one line dividing the panel into one-third and two-thirds we had come to grips with all the elements.

*The Cartoon*

In Figure 16-2, our actual working cartoon, you can see that we were not entirely satisfied with the lines even at this stage. However, modifications were all in the background; an example of the divisional schizophrenia that many designers go through right into the final stages. This is usually due to staring at the thing too long.

At this stage, the three portions of the panel are clear enough. The top third shows the nameplate line enhanced by painted detail into a scroll being pulled by the heraldic bull below. Notice how the linear quality of the scroll is carried to right and left by the painted lines. The bull is to be indicated rather than ornately painted, since we didn't want to diffuse the power of the coat of arms in the center. This central section will contain the most spectacular glass in the panel; it will be the area the eye hits first. Above it we have the separatist area, the pause between the two pictures. We decided to use small pieces of glass here to further slow down the eye.

The lower third will contain a motto in French which could apply to the entire conception. Again note how painted lines used in this area mold the basic linear quality into a flowing scroll arrangement. The eye forgets the blocked lines and follows the picture; it's the job of the designer to make it do exactly that.

THE PATTERN

We cut all pieces of the central pattern with a $1/16''$ pattern scissors; the rest with a $1/8''$. We intend to use heavy leads out-

173

side the shield; thinner leads within. When cutting any pattern for a panel containing painted detail, it's a good idea to remember which line is painted and which is cut. Never number paint lines or you may cut them by mistake. In Figure 16-3, we show the pattern being cut and replaced on the underlying cartoon. The painted bull is not shown in the pattern but we see the painted hand. Only the cut lines of the dagger are shown.

It is imperative that all pieces be cut exactly since we intend to matt paint all the background. Often you can jog a piece a little with a glass cutter or grozing pliers if it doesn't fit in the leading; however, once glass is fired, it tends to acquire rounded edges which are difficult to groze or score away. You may break a piece of glass that doesn't fit properly. If that happens to a painted piece you have to recut, repaint and rebake it; an operation that can hold up your work for 24 hours.

Fig. 16-2 The final cartoon . . . essentially.

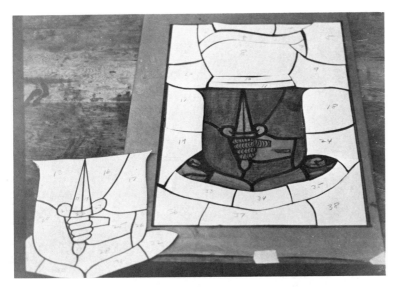

Fig. 16-3   The pattern being
cut.

## CUTTING THE GLASS

As in any project in this craft, cut all glass and make sure it fits
together before doing anything else. We know individuals who
cut and lead their glass as one operation. We feel there is only
one type of project where that is advisable (see Chap. 18, Glass
Galleon). In most instances, it can be disastrous. You can't be
certain your colors will work and can't tell what effect your total
conception will promote. By laying out your pieces, you grasp a
totality invisible to the piece-worker.

In Figure 16-4, you see the pieces of glass cut and laid out over
the light table. They present the usual blank look; the linear outline is blurred and the painted details are missing with only the
color blending or marring, according to how well or ill we've calculated. Color is what's important at this stage—assuming, of
course, that your cutting has been accurate.

## THE PAINTED DETAIL

In Figure 16-5, we want to show the painted sketch of the
bull. Even the finished product is not meant to be ornate. The
outline of the bull has been done in thick paint lines; these are
being slimmed by means of a stick-light. (Details of painting
techniques will be found in Chap. 4.) With glass painting, it is
easier to take paint away than add; in most instances, it is next to
impossible to add.

The modifications made by the stick-light are more readily
seen in Figure 16-6. Here the bull appears shaven but essential,
with the outlines focused and in perspective. Also note here the
finger painting and the dagger. We changed our mind about a

175

Fig. 16-4 The glass cut to pattern.

cut line here and substituted a paint line. Note the outline of the scroll above and below. Compare this with Figure 16-4. Look how much design life has been added.

In Figure 16-7, the bull is presented after it has been matted (shadowed) with the requisite brush strokes (see Chap. 4 for painting techniques). We fired several bulls before we got one we felt was right for the panel; this wasn't the one. The matting here is overdone and the scroll lines are "fired"—that is, broken up

176

Fig. 16-5 Molding the paint lines of the bull to final form.

Fig. 16-6 Beginning painting on the glass; trace lines only.

177

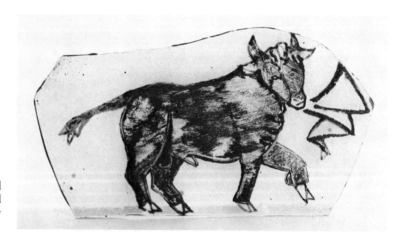

Fig. 16-7 A poor painted result. Lines are "fried" and the texture is much too heavy and blurred.

and shriveled from the heat of the kiln. The perspective is correct, however.

The lettering in this panel can be done freehand or with a stencil. If you are going to be doing repetitive lettering, it's probably best to screen it. We did the lettering freehand. Since the glass was a transparent antique grey, we placed the letters beneath it and painted directly on the glass guided from the outline below. Spacing is critical here and, unless you have a bit of practice in lettering, it's best to cut the letters from whatever guide you're using and paste them into the actual words. Secure this to the bottom of the glass with cellophane tape and try not to drop any paint next to it. If this happens, the drip will ooze between the glass and the paper and smudge the whole works. You then cheerfully start all over.

A repeat caution about glass painting: make absolutely certain the glass is clean before you paint and clean the underside before firing. Careless specks of paint left here will fire into the glass as well as your intended artwork and will end up drawing more attention.

LEADING UP

As with any panel this is a standard operation, but consideration must be given to painted areas that run from one piece of glass onto the next as in the scroll areas. These pieces must match exactly; nothing looks sillier and more amateurish than paint lines that don't meet. All the leading must fit precisely; a small discrepancy in one area can show up grossly in another painted area. Figure 16-8 shows the lead knife being used to snug a piece of H lead against the upper curve of glass. Figure 16-9 shows the panel being leaded. The background pieces are locked as far as the painted sections to the right and below. All leading is done over the work drawing; never freehand.

178

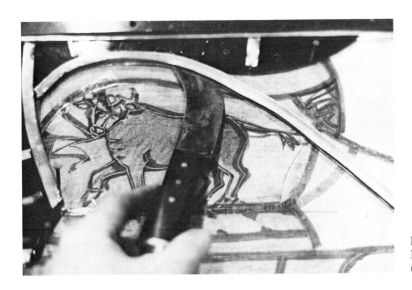

Fig. 16-8 Leading begun.
Note how the lead knife is
used to seat the came.

Fig. 16-9 Showing the
leading process in operation.

179

Fig. 16-10 The leaded
panel completed. (See color
section and Fig. A-3)

Figure 16-10 shows the completely leaded panel. Here is the
matting of the background. The different sizes of the leading are
apparent and the phrase in French reads "Dieu et Droit." The
last word is split by a lead line; a circumstance that many designers avoid and which we generally do not allow. It would have
been little trouble to recut this piece of glass. We did not because
we wanted the panel to appear old (medieval craftsmen were no-
toriously careless with their lead lines), and we wanted to show
what a word split by a lead line looks like. Even for an eye that
doesn't know the language, it should be obvious from the spacing
of the other words that this is a complete word—lead line or not.
It's not quite the same to the eye as having a picture design split
by a lead line but your eye does stop for a moment. We would not
advise treating every word like this; this kind of novelty is easily
overdone. "Negative painting" is shown for the curved portions

of the scroll. Here the background glass was blacked out, allowing the grey to stand as a positive image. This is just the opposite to the technique used on the bull.

CLEANING UP

The basic cleaning up process has been covered in "How to Work in Stained Glass" but we will review it very quickly here. The paint won't come off the glass no matter how hard you scrub with cleaning agents, but you will be able to remove the grime. Putty is inserted under the lead came with the fingers. This serves a two-fold purpose of stiffening the lead and acting as a sponge to remove flux oxides from the glass and joints. When the putty has been inserted, the lead flanges are turned down with a putty knife and excess putty removed. The window can then be cleaned with cleaning and polishing powder and a scrub brush.

# 17 Chapter

# THE SUNFLOWER

This project introduces the technique of using glass bends for purposes other than lampshade panels. By using small pieces of glass foiled together in Tiffany-fashion, dimensional curves can be exhibited. While in no way negating the usefulness of this method, certain objects must provide a more unbroken sweep and curl. Single curved pieces of glass prepared in the kiln are essential to express this linear longing. Certain challenges present themselves in this type of fabrication.

THE DESIGN

A sunflower in a vase is the subject. We want to present the sunflower with curved petals and the vase broken with a curled leaf protruding from the distressed surface. All curves will be bent glass pieces. For the original drawing in Figure 17-1, we use two dimensions, however, indicating the curl of the petals. The petals will also have paint lines on their surfaces and the middle portion of the flower, to correspond to the seeds, should have a rough surface of some sort. The two leaves shown will be straight glass. The third leaf will be added later.

The vase furnished more problems design-wise than the flower, which was a fairly straightforward object. There are any number of ways to present this container. We settled for the lines as shown which we felt balanced out pretty well. Not shown in this basic sketch is the sum of the curves of these pieces rising to the center so that, when completed, the vase would form a partial semicircle with the flower inside it. But all of this is yet to come; the first steps are standard.

MAKING THE PATTERN

Once you are satisfied with your design, cut your pattern in the usual manner. Since we are going to be foiling all portions of

Fig. 17-1 The Sunflower
cartoon.

Fig. 17-2   The pattern being cut.

this object, a regular scissors is used to cut the pieces of pattern paper. These are placed back onto the original drawing to make sure they fit properly (see Fig. 17-2). We decided to first provide the vase; based on its shape and size, we would then do the flower. It is important when designing for curved glass to fabricate one section of the design at a time. No matter how good it may look in the "flat," once the curved pieces are put together they may provide a different perspective and you must work other portions of the design against them. Figure 17-3 shows the cut pieces of

Fig. 17-3 The glass cut to pattern.

opalescent glass (opalescent is really demanded here) in position against the original sketch. They all fit quite well.

MAKING THE FORM

Utilizing the shape of the vase with no breaks for glass design, we trace out its borders on a piece of sheet metal (see Fig. 17-4). The design is cut from the metal with a pair of shears so that we have a flat, metallic (and rather uninteresting) template. You might notice how much is added to this bland surface by the break lines shown in the original design. This metal pattern, unassuming as it is, will become a critical factor in the final result so cut it carefully and smooth all edges with a file or Carborundum paper.

Next trace the break lines onto it in heavy ink just the way they fall in the design (see Fig. 17-5). This is necessary to give a sense of proportion when it comes to molding the curve of the vase as well as to provide a realistic appraisal of how each individual piece will be bent. Figure 17-5 shows the template hand molded into a curve with the design in place as shown by the original drawing to the left. The curve is a moderate one for two

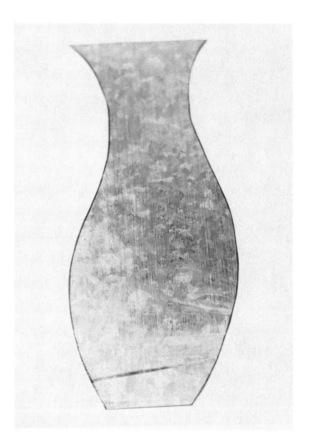

Fig. 17-4 The sheet metal template, flat.

reasons: the design is not meant to be half a vase but only to indicate such and the clay mold we will make from this form cannot be too steep along the sides or the glass pieces will fall off. At this stage, we have not yet decided where the broken part of the vase will be; we do know that one of the top pieces will not be placed to provide this representation. The form measures 17″ long and is 3½″ across at the base. At its widest it is 7″ across, dipping in to 4″ at the neck and flowering out to 6″ at the top.

MAKING THE MOLD

We are going to use red terra cotta clay for this mold. Take a hefty amount and work it into a mound roughly equal to twice the size of the metal form. Because of the size of our kiln, we found the form would be too large for placement of the mold the way we wanted it—a good 3″ to 4″ away from the firebrick on all sides—so we cut the form along the lower neck line. Although this necessitated two separate firings, it gave us more room to maneuver the mold and hence the glass pieces within the kiln. It is also easier to make a clay mold from a form which does not provide such long curves all at once. Since the metal must be im-

Fig. 17-5 The sheet metal template, curved to make the mold with break lines inked in as shown in the original drawing alongside.

pressed into the clay base, there is always the danger these long curves may tend to flatten more readily than short ones. We had considered this possibility from the start and placed the two parallel neck lines for just this purpose.

With the two pieces of the form ready, each is pressed firmly into a mound of clay, leaving a negative impression. The ridges formed by the borders of the form are smoothed away and the clay, as yet unfired, is placed in the kiln and covered with a fine layer of kiln wash. It is now ready for use.

There are two things to bear in mind before going any further. The first is that you may wish to fire your clay mold before attempting to use it with glass. That way if it falls apart, you haven't wasted any glass. However, we feel this wastes time. If you exercise care in making your mold, you shouldn't have trouble here. Which brings up the second point: to indeed exercise such care! Clay molds fall apart because the clay was not kneaded properly, it was put into the kiln cold without any warming process to overcome the thermal shock, air bubbles were trapped within it, the kiln was not vented properly, or any one of a half dozen other reasons all of which may be overcome by reading a book about clay, kilns and molds. We find that by working the clay to the proper softness and pliability, we have always been able to fire the glass and the clay together with very few problems.

BENDING THE VASE PIECES

Figure 17-6 shows the bottom mold within the kiln with the corresponding pieces of glass placed over it preparatory to firing. Two of the right lower pieces have been left off the mold to show its surface covered with kiln wash. You can see here what we meant earlier about the steepness of the sides; it wouldn't take much more curvature to unsettle the glass. Once the two missing pieces are added, we will turn the kiln to low heat and put the top down, leaving a 2" space at the bottom so the heated air within may escape. This is called venting the kiln; it doesn't take long—10 minutes, perhaps—and it helps provide fewer accidents within. Once the kiln has been vented, the top is closed and the heat allowed to rise to between 1250° and 1300°F. At this temperature, most opalescent glass bends.

As we pointed out in our book on stained glass lamps, we rarely allow slow cooling of glass. Once the proper temperature has been reached, we open the kiln wide, allowing the heat to dissipate rapidly. The advantage to this is obvious in time saving. Not all glass can be so treated, however, as we will point out when we discuss bending the flower petals.

In Figure 17-7, we see the pieces of bent glass now foiled and

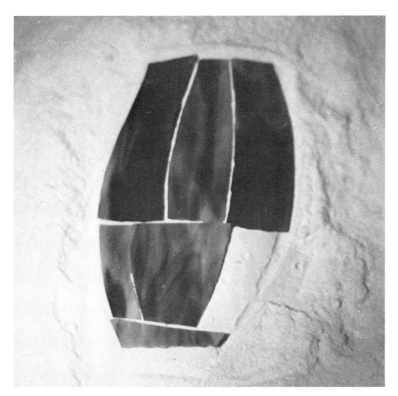

Fig. 17-6 The glass pieces on the mold in the kiln. They are balanced very precariously.

replaced on the original design. Notice how closely the pieces still fit—both to their neighboring pieces and to the underlying conception. This is more important than with flat glass projects where a piece may be shaved to fit or even recut along the way. To recut a piece here would mean rebending it somewhere along the mold surface out of relationship to the other pieces. While relationship can be established by putting all the other pieces back on the mold and then removing them, leaving only the piece to be rebent, it's a lot of work. It's much better to cut all pieces accurately at first. This final check does allow any miscut bent piece to be picked up before the final locking up process of soldering. You can also see in Figure 17-7 that we have decided where the broken portion of the vase will be—directly opposite the inner leaf in the drawing.

PLACING THE LEAVES

We have determined there will be one bent leaf and two straight ones. One of the straight leaves will rise out of the vase at the area of the planned break; the bent leaf will curl down from this same area with its point soldered to one of the lead lines of the vase. Figure 17-8 shows these two leaves in place and, at the right, the piece of copper form used to make the mold

189

Projects

Fig. 17-7   The bent pieces of glass, foiled and placed back on the pattern to check position and size.

for the bent leaf. The straight leaf fills the space in the top of the vase; the bent leaf's upper end is soldered to the lead lines at this area. We used a copper form and a plaster mold for the bent leaf since we needed a finer casting than clay allows. Note in Figure 17-8 how the pieces of the vase fit together so that the two long curves to either side have been maintained exactly as called for by the design.

MAKING THE FLOWER

*The Petals*

We decided to make the petals out of yellow opalescent glass. These were cut according to the design specifications but when it came to bending them we couldn't see the necessity for providing separate molds. Instead we decided to utilize those molds we already had for the body of the vase. By placing the petals along

190

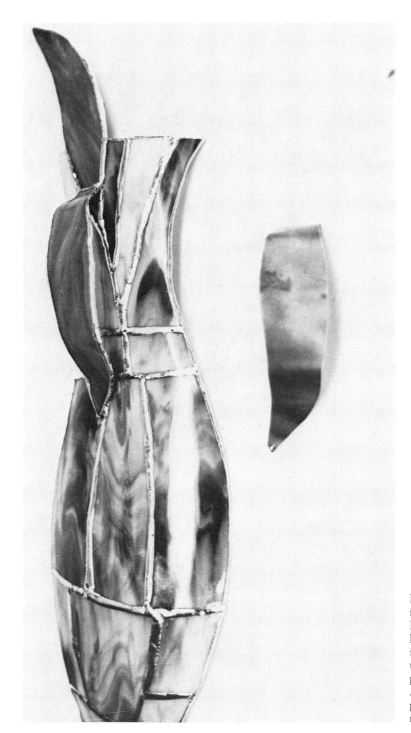

Fig. 17-8 The vase pieces foiled and soldered to shape. Evenness of the border curves has been maintained. The flat leaf has been added up top and the curved leaf placed over the vase surface. Alongside is the copper template from which the plaster mold was made.

Fig. 17-9    The curved petals placed back on the pattern to check size and position.

their outer curved sides, it was possible to bend them to just the right shape (see Fig. 17-9). While we were congratulating ourselves on the time saved, we heard ominous sounds from the kiln which we had, as usual, thrown open as soon as the glass hit the correct temperature. These pingings meant the glass was cooling irregularly and starting to fragment; yellow opalescent apparently is touchy as to contraction coefficients. Alone among all the types and hues of glass we've worked with, yellow opalescent must be stone cold when it comes from the kiln—and even then it may ruffle into layers and shed portions of its surface like pieces of mica. Unfortunately, it's the best color for petals and we did finally get them all bent and arranged on the drawing for painting (see Fig. 17-10).

Painting involved placing a black line down the center of each piece. In Figure 17-10, the drawing is on the light table and the pieces of glass have been painted, foiled and are being soldered together. Painting can be done either before or after the pieces have been bent. If after, it is silly to refire, so use a Talens® paint which stays on quite well even without heat; if before, the glass is

Fig. 17-10 The petals painted and beginning to be soldered into place.

painted and then fired so the bending and sealing of the paint takes place in one kiln firing.

### The Center

The seeded area of the center called for a more textured, irregular surface than any granite backed glass we could offer. We decided on an orange, semi-transparent center amidst all those yellow petals (some of which were still pinging) and accordingly selected the reddist antique we could find, knowing it would fade to orange by the time it reached temperature. This was not bending temperature—the center piece remains straight—but fusing temperature. We decided to use crushed glass here and to imbed it to look like seeds (see Fig. 17-11). This would also give us our semi-transparent effect.

In Figure 17-12, we can see the final effect of the elements composing the flower, including the stem. Note the way the petal bends fit together even though they were not draped over specific molds. This combining mold technique has been used by us for many bent projects and saves a lot of time and energy. You

193

Fig. 17-11 The central portion of the flower covered with crushed glass prior to fusing.

can also see the roughened effect the fused glass gives the center; this effect is more noticeable in Figures 17-13 and 17-14.

*The Stem*

The stem is composed of two elements: the stem proper and the holding bar. The stem proper is a 1¾″ piece of ½″ lead. It is covered with solder on all surfaces and supports nothing; it is there strictly for show.

The basic support of the flower is the holding bar which is not seen from the front. It extends from the top of the flower to the

Fig. 17-12 The flower put together. Note the two portions of the stem.

194

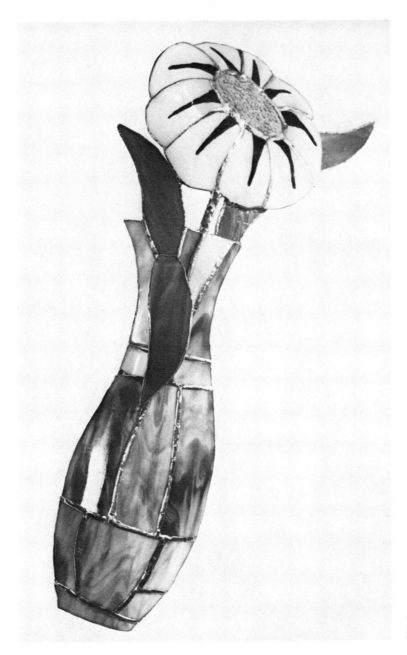

Fig. 17-13 The completed Sunflower, hung and back lit.

upper line of the vase. It is soldered to the upper flower rim, spans the inside curve of the flower and is soldered to the lower flower rim behind the stem and thence to the lead lines behind the vase. It is a ¼″ piece of galvanized steel placed for maximum support along its thin surface. The top-heavy flower is prevented from any side to side swing by attachment on the left to the straight leaf we have described and on the right by the long leaf we will not describe.

195

Fig. 17-14 The completed Sunflower, hung and lit from the front. (See color section)

*The Long Leaf*

This is a new leaf but we're not going to turn it over; we've already done one to that purpose. This one is in two parts. The first comes out of the right top of the vase and spans a distance of 1¼" to attach behind the flower's bottom rim. This portion furnishes the actual support. The second portion of this leaf is at-

196

tached behind the top right hand rim of the flower to give the illusion of a single growth. If we were to actually make this all one piece we would not be able to use this leaf as well for flower support and it would also cast a shadow behind the flower that we don't want. Figure 17-13 and Figure 17-14 show the completed flower lighted from the front and the back.

# 18 Chapter

# GLASS GALLEON

For the final project in this book, we wanted to come up with something truly spectacular; we think you'll agree we've succeeded. We ask that you do not attempt this one until you have acquainted yourself with most of the other projects and techniques discussed; many of them have a bearing on this last voyage and your chances of making the most of this composition will be measured by your understanding of much of what has come before.

BEFORE YOU BEGIN

As you get ready to begin this masterpiece of a project, we have a few suggestions to help you along the way.

1. Use opalescent glass throughout. The hull should be one color, the gun deck another and the decks and sides a third.

2. You must make the basic shape large enough to accommodate all the smaller shapes within it. Otherwise, there will be an awful lot of crowding. You can make the basic shape as large as you like, however, without adding any extra pieces; simply make the pieces described proportionately larger.

3. Don't attempt too much at any one time. As you overwork, the first thing that goes is your self-criticism. It's better to do a little correctly than to do a lot at once and do it poorly.

4. You may wish to add other sails or deck furniture; there is some room for both. Remember there is a point when you will be defeating your purpose, which is to make each aspect add to the overall effect. The more you add, the more gets hidden.

5. If you have a project of this nature in mind, save all opalescent scraps from other projects. Minimal size pieces are required here.

6. As for placing a light in the hull—don't do it. This would cheapen the design and make your audience miss the boat!

*The Ship from the Side*

Any picture of a full rigged sailing ship under sail will give you an idea of where we are going. We will end up with exactly such a ship in three dimensional stained glass, riding on its own ocean.

Let's begin from the bottom up with Figure 18-1. Here we have drawn the basic shape of the hull. This measures 10″ in length and is 2¼″ at its widest and 2″ at its narrowest width. This pattern must be drawn and cut twice, one being the reverse of the other; when matched together, they will form the two sides of the ship's bottom. We will come back to this.

The top drawing in Figure 18-1 shows the relationships of the rest of the ship to the hull as seen from the side. The *gun deck* area is composed of eight pieces of glass approximately 1½″ apart directly atop the upper line of the hull. There are spaces (blackened in the drawing) of ½″ between these glass pieces through which the guns will point. The front and back (or fore and aft) glass pieces are of different sizes from the middle ones. This is because of the curve of the hull; this spatial modification must be kept in mind throughout the construction of the ship. The front piece of glass rises up and around to make the turn of the bow which also dips in slightly as it meets the centerline; that's the reason for the break line near the front. This break line helps keep a graceful flow line with the bow. The back piece of glass is squarecut and meets directly with the stern. Of course, all these glass pieces are exactly duplicated on the other side of the bow.

*Two stern plates* must be cut; one for each side. There are a number of sharp angles here; try to cut them just that way. This, second only to the bow, is the piece that most gives the ship its familiar shape. If the back angles are sluffed, you will end up with one long curve from upper deck to bow—not the silhouette we want at all. If the front angles are too smooth, the distinction of the decks will blur and the ornamentation will all run together. This piece measures 4½″ long at the bottom and is 2¼″ high at the upper deck.

You need to cut two *center plates*. The center plate measures 3″ along the bottom and 3½″ across the top. The top of this piece will represent the lower deck.

There are two *prow plates* representing an original single plate that had to be split in order to make the curve of the bow. The technique used here is similar to that in a small pieced lamp where small straight pieces of glass are angled to make the bend.

You will note in Figure 18-1 that there seems to be a lot of room between the pieces we have discussed. Also these pieces

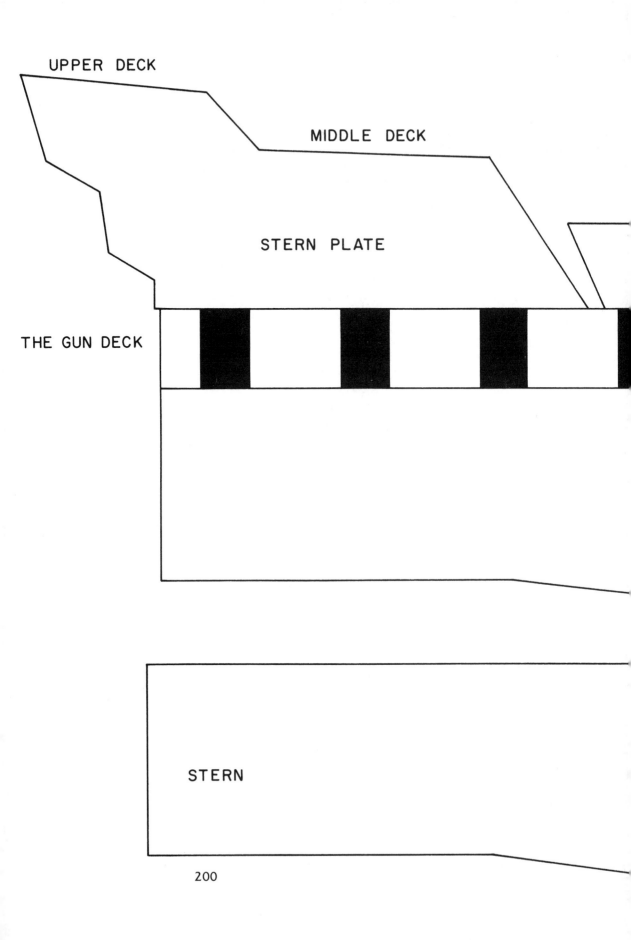

UPPER DECK

MIDDLE DECK

STERN PLATE

THE GUN DECK

STERN

200

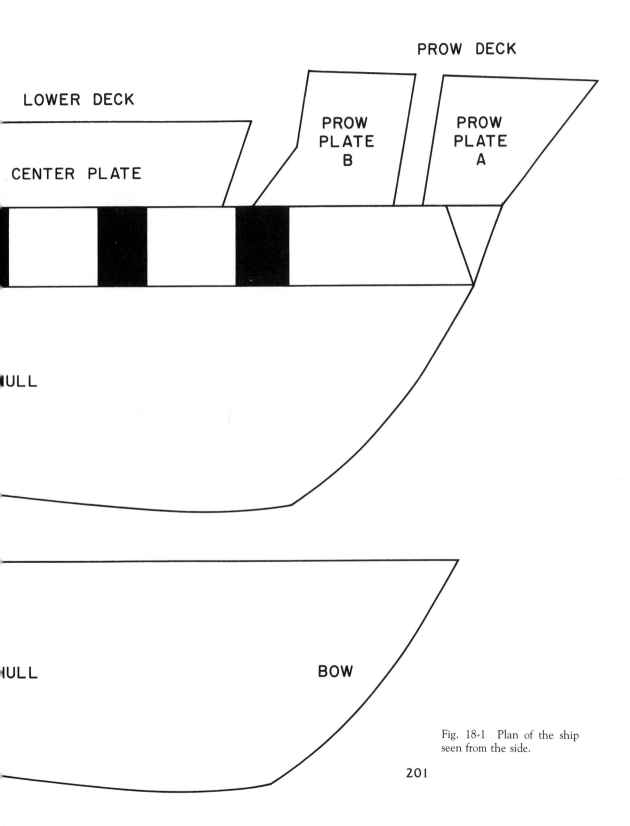

Fig. 18-1 Plan of the ship seen from the side.

don't appear to be designed to fit together precisely. This would all be a terrible designing mistake if we were discussing a flat piece of glass for the bow, with ancillary elements sitting atop it to give us only a side view. Once the bow becomes curved, it foreshortens and the space between pieces, as well as the relationship of the pieces to each other, will change. So follow exactly the lines we have drawn; you'll be surprised how readily your pieces will go together when the time comes.

*The Ship from Above*

In Figure 18-2, we are looking at the ship from above. There are four major portions of deck each separated from the next by a wall (strut). The two sides are formed from the pieces we have just discussed (see Figure 18-1). Between the prow and the lower deck, the separating wall is straight up and down; from the side, it is the vertical back part of prow plate B. Between the lower deck and the middle deck the wall is slanted; from the side it is the front line of the stern plate. From the middle deck to the upper deck, the wall is again on a slant; from the side it is the upper center line of the stern plate. All these decks are further indicated, as was mentioned before, by the back lines of the stern plate.

Looking at the design of the ship from above, it is a good idea to consider how evenly the decks are to be cut. Unless the three back rectangles and the front triangle are maintained so they fit together evenly, your ship will founder. We have designed these pieces so they fit within the sides, not on top of them; this is true also of the walls between them.

*The Ship from Behind*

The essentially symmetrical outline of the project is again brought forth by this view in Figure 18-3 of the center pieces. The three upper decks correspond on side view to the angled vertical back portions of the stern plate; the separations between them to the horizontal portions of this same piece. It follows, therefore, that if this plate is cut exactly even on both sides, you can't miss when you get to this part; all you have to do is follow the angles indicated. Probably the most trouble you will have is getting the back of the hull quite as even as is shown here. Due to the curve of the hull, this piece is not quite as much under your control as the other flat pieces of glass. You may have to work a little on this flat back portion of the hull to compensate for slight irregularities along the sides in which it must fit. Work a little at a time, trying always not to groze so much off one edge that the symmetry will be destroyed.

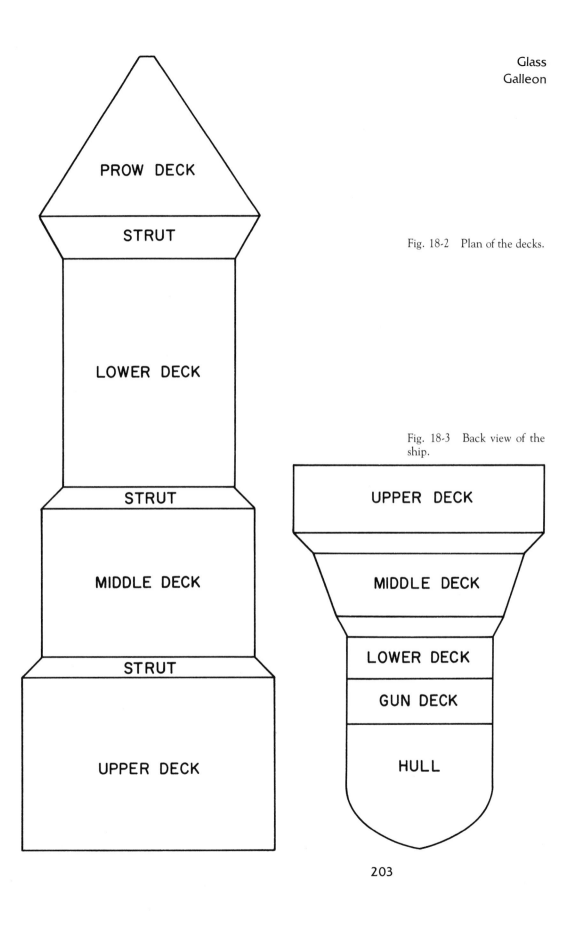

PROW DECK

STRUT

LOWER DECK

STRUT

MIDDLE DECK

STRUT

UPPER DECK

Fig. 18-2    Plan of the decks.

Fig. 18-3    Back view of the ship.

UPPER DECK

MIDDLE DECK

LOWER DECK

GUN DECK

HULL

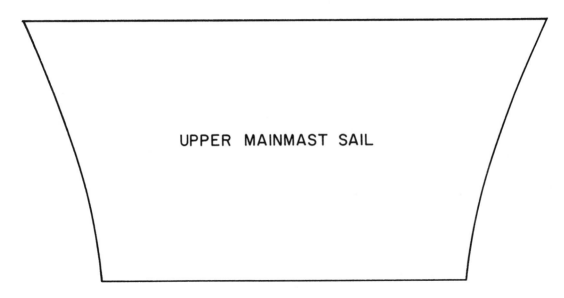

Fig. 18-4   Plan of the sails.

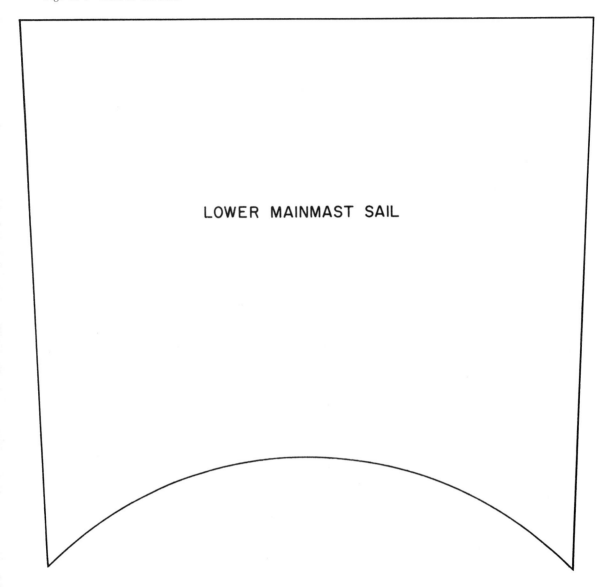

There are six sails of varying sizes and shapes for this ship (see Figs. 18-4 to 18-6). They will each be curved in the kiln to a special form which has been calculated into the overall design. Don't skimp here; you may feel a tendency to use bent sails similar to the Sailboat project; they will look terrible. Cut all your sail patterns as we have given them here; the sails will be just about the last thing you will add. You can cut them now if you wish, but don't worry about them yet.

THE COPPER MOCK UP

Sheet copper is required of a thickness sufficient to allow it to hold a shape firmly but not so thick as to make it unworkable with the hands. You can try using sheet metal, as we did in the Sunflower project, but for the comparatively small sizes of some of the objects to be bent in comparison to the large, gradual bend of the sunflower vase, you might find sheet metal a little too springy. We prefer copper; you can acquire sheets of it in some hobby shops. If you have a sheet of copper that you're afraid is too thin to hold a shape adequately, try tinning it on both sides. This will stiffen it and may just do the trick for you. Be sure the tinning is even, however, without any lumps and bumps of solder which will otherwise impress into the mold.

For this reason, once you get your copper, you must make certain it is absolutely flat. Hammer it out on a good firm surface. We keep a piece of steel girder for this and pound away with a large rubber mallet (see Fig. 18-7). As you progress with your flattening, you will find the copper curling up somewhat along the surface you are whacking; turn it over and apply more of the same. It shouldn't take more than a few minutes to have a nice flat piece of metal which, in addition to being bumpless, will also be more malleable.

Against this flat surface, trace the outlines of both sides of the hull previously cut from pattern paper and cut them out with a pair of shears. Using your fingers, mold them into the curves as seen in Figure 18-8. You must make each side as exact a duplicate of the other as possible. Unfortunately, you can't mold the pieces together since the curvatures are opposite to each other, but you will be surprised how close you can come to identical shaping nonetheless. One of the major problems with making side to side curves in a piece of metal while also attempting up and down ones is the amount of creases and bumps that can occur as the two curves cross. Work out of this by recurving an inch or so at a time. Your fingers are your best tool here. Use the thumb for pressing and the rest of the fingers for gradual pulling. The best way to avoid getting into trouble is to make haste

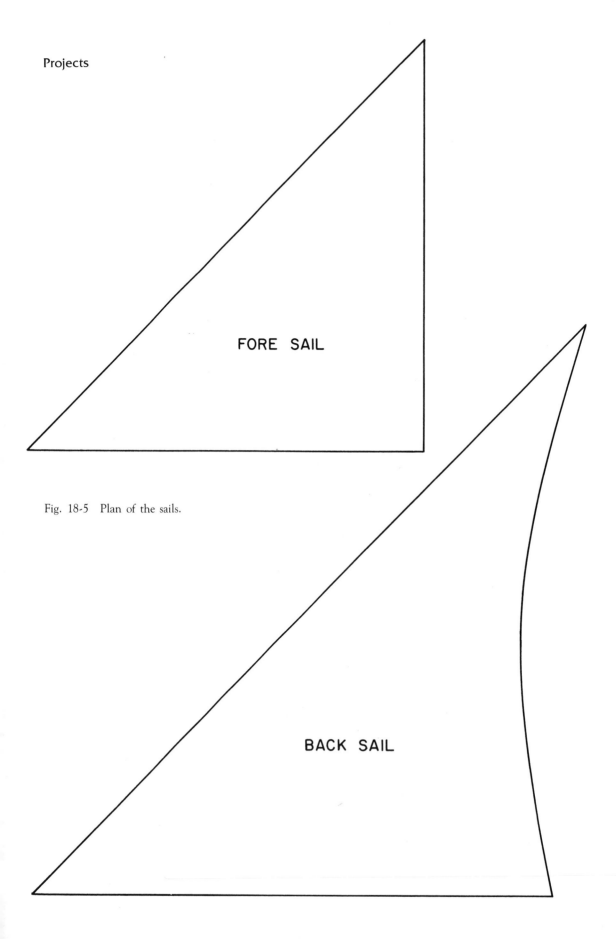

FORE SAIL

Fig. 18-5 Plan of the sails.

BACK SAIL

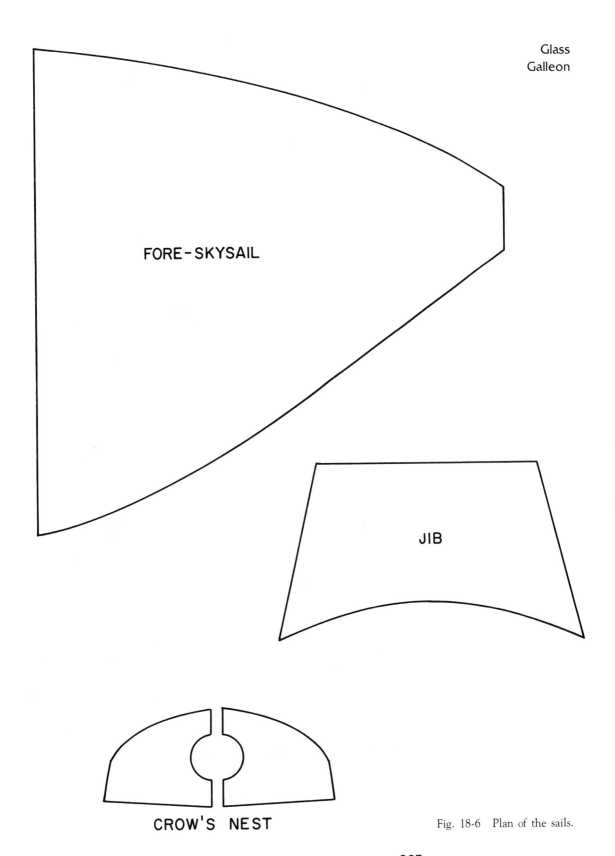

FORE-SKYSAIL

JIB

CROW'S NEST

Fig. 18-6  Plan of the sails.

Fig. 18-7 Flattening the metal for use as forms from which to make molds.

slowly. Allow a good hour to get both pieces of the hull to match. Figure 18-9 shows how our match of both sides turned out. We put both pieces of hull together and taped them to the table so we could stand back and get a perspective. The side to side curve is pretty even down the length of the piece until the bow curve begins to take over. It flattens out a little here but there's no way to force it beyond this without creasing the metal. The other side, seen across the top, looks pretty good. Again look at Figure 18-8 for a comparison of the two sides.

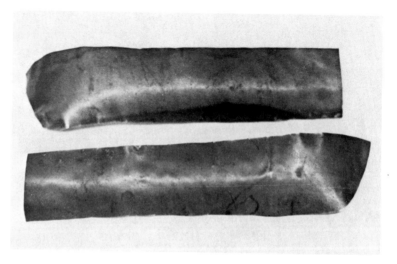

Fig. 18-8 Copper forms for the hull.

Fig. 18-9 The two portions of the copper hull placed together to show the identity of the sides.

We are rarely satisfied with our copper mock-ups; you may have the same problem. All the same, you can go only so far; beyond that point you are wasting time. When that point comes, it is time to turn to the next step.

MAKING THE MOLD

In a rubber mixing bowl, prepare a moderate setting plaster. This should be turned to a creamy consistency with your spatula. Once this point is reached, the mixture is poured directly into the copper form. Figure 18-10 shows the mixture going into one of the sail forms but the same principle is followed for the hull. Both copper hull forms should be filled with the plaster. We use this method rather than the clay we used for the Sunflower mold because our curvature tolerances are more important here. Do not make the plaster so loose that it will run out the ends of the mold, nor so thick that it won't pour.

When the plaster is within the copper form, tap the sides of the form with your spatula to break loose any air bubbles that

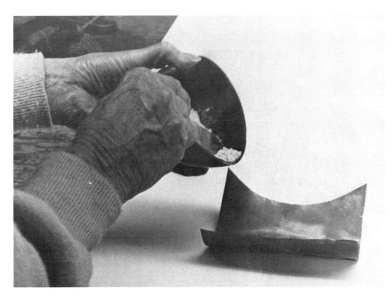

Fig. 18-10 Demonstrating how to pour plaster into a copper form.

209

may have gotten inside. We work mostly with dental plaster; you can acquire three types: fast, medium and slow setting. A dental supply company will furnish you with what you need. This plaster is well suited to take extremely high heat.

While the plaster is setting, it gets quite hot. Wait until it is cool, turn the form over carefully and lift it off. The only time you will have trouble getting the copper form away from the plaster is if you have inadvertently undercut the copper. This is another reason to make sure your copper sheet is smooth and without nicks or bends along the edges.

Coat the plaster with a release material. Kay Kinney's Mold Coat® is a good one; or you can sift kiln wash to get out any lumps or foreign material, make a loose paste of it and paint that on. Your mold is ready for firing.

FIRING THE GLASS

Before you can fire the glass, you have to position your mold in the kiln. This is not as easy as it sounds with this project. Many of the pieces to be made are irregular and the hull molds won't stand up properly to allow the glass to drape. So clean all kiln wash out of the kiln and use a flat shelf to support the hull molds. As you see in Figure 18-11, the copper forms corresponding to these molds assume a side position when left to themselves; the molds may do the same. You have to get them upright—that is resting on the front point and the back semicircle. Kiln furniture, shelf spacers or anything that will take the heat and support the mold in the position you want it will help here. Calculate this support with care, otherwise the weight of the glass slumping over the mold will knock it over and make a mess. Once you have your molds arranged, cut glass to the size of your paper pattern and lay it atop the mold so that when it drapes it will fall where you want it. This should occur at 1250°F but we like to peek into the kiln (we always use a top loader for this purpose) to make sure sagging has occurred properly.

Fig. 18-11 Copper forms used in this project.

*Putting the Frame Together*

When the glass has cooled, you should have two pieces bent to the shape of your original copper hulls. Foil all edges with ¼″ adhesive back copper, taking care, especially at the bends, to get the foil even on both sides. Then tack the two sides of the hull together at the inner seam first and the inside of the prow second. If you are satisfied that the two sides are as even as possible, do a firm soldering job. Cut the back side of the hull and foil and solder it in place. The hull will now look something like a large canoe.

*Adding the Gun Deck*

In Figure 18-12, you can see how the small pieces of glass forming the gun deck are being added to the top of the hull. Each of these fifteen pieces has been foiled with ³/₁₆″ tape and soldered evenly into place. The back piece fits within the two side pieces. One way to make sure your glass pieces are in matching position across the hull is to take a spacer—a flat bar about ½″ wide will do—and lay it across the hull. Then solder the glass in place on both sides to either side of the spacer. These glass pieces must be as firmly placed as possible, especially since you are going to be adding additional glass pieces on top of them. If they begin to waver, you'll have all sorts of difficulties.

*Adding the Stern Plates*

The two stern plates are now added to the top of the back portion of the gun deck, taking up completely the tops of the back three pieces of glass and about half of the fourth piece (see Fig. 18-13). The back of each stern plate should be in line with the back of the last piece of glass which in turn is lined up with the back of the hull.

It is likely you'll have more trouble with the large stern plates wobbling on their lower solder joint than you did with the plates

Fig. 18-12 The glass hull pieces soldered together and the pieces of the gun deck soldered in place.

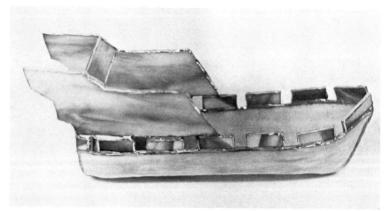

Fig. 18-13 The two stern plates shown soldered in place. The first deck plate forms the strut between them.

of the gun deck. If your foiling is loose at any point, these plates may fall over. Foiling here is difficult because of the severe angulations of the back, so take your time putting copper around these pieces. Solder inside the hull as well as outside and have the first strut to go across cut and foiled and ready for immediate placement before soldering the stern plates. This first strut (see Figs. 18-3 and 18-13) will form the angled wall to the upper deck previously discussed.

It may prove a little tricky holding these pieces for soldering, but if you use your belly to hold the ship hull at the proper angle, you can solder the further stern plate at the inside line. Now, supporting the hull by the partially soldered stern plate, roll it toward you and solder the outside line.

Turn the hull around and repeat the process for the other stern plate. It's at this point that you'll find that your lower gun deck plates had better be solid. Next, holding the ends of the stern plates apart with the back three fingers of your left hand, support the first strut with the first two fingers and solder it in place. This will immediately strengthen the entire complex. Now take the time to solder everything firmly and check if any of the foil is coming loose. If it is, iron it down with the soldering iron.

*Adding the Center and Prow Plates*

The center plate continues along the straight line of the gun deck to the corner of the bow. It takes up the half bottom glass on the gun deck left by the stern plate and another piece and a half before it meets the first of the prow plates. It is an easy piece to solder because it is supported from below by the gun deck plates and from behind by the stern plate (see Fig. 18-14).

The two prow plates form the curve of the bow and must be angled with care against each other but still follow the line below. The front bow plate must also meet its cousin flush on the opposite side. If you look carefully at Figure 18-14, you will no-

Fig. 18-14 The stern plate, the center plate and the two prow plates soldered into place. The gun deck takes shape and stability once these pieces are put together.

tice that if you were to drop a perpendicular from the upper margin of the picture to the point of the hull, another to the fur-thest foreward glass piece of the gun deck and a third to the point of the first prow plate, these lines would be spaced considerably apart. In other words, we have purposely extended the prow a little further with each layer; again this is necessary because of that foreward curve. The slight discrepancies in glass that are unavoidable here can be filled in with solder.

The ultimate design goal is to throw that front bow upward and outward; a simple matter if we were cutting a single piece of glass in one dimension, but somewhat more involved when dealing with three dimensions. Now all the side pieces fit and the hull begins to look a little more like a boat and less like a canoe.

*Tidying Up the Gun Ports*

Take a look at Figure 18-15. The ship is laid on its side so we may work on the openings between the gun deck plates. Initially,

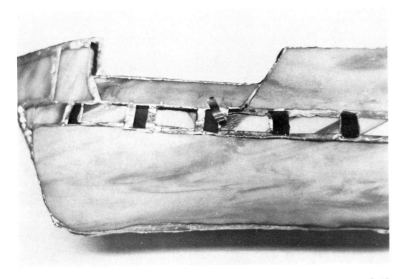

Fig. 18-15 Preparing the gun ports. These are evened with pieces of copper foil.

they are just ragged holes formed by the glass around them. We must give them a character of their own and make them ports. This is done with the ubiquitous copper foil.

Cut small strands of ¼″ foil and place them flat around the openings as shown. Solder them to the lines above and below. Note the difference that this presents in evening out the spaces from that on the left to the two on the right still to be foiled.

In Figure 18-16, we see how all the spaces look with the foiled border placed. The lower line has also had copper tape stretched along its length and has been partially beaded. A similar line of tape will be stretched on top and then all the surfaces will be beaded (see Fig. 18-17). The beading (a process of soldering to a raised, rounded edge) will take place with little trouble if you remember (1) to flux the copper well; (2) use plenty of solder; (3) use a clean iron and don't try to push the solder, let it mount up and flow on its own. The beading can only be done with the ship on its side. All presenting copper lines are so treated at this time.

*Placing the Deck Plates*

Figure 18-17 shows the completed basic ship. All surfaces are smoothly beaded and the deck plates have been cut and soldered. The first deck plate was the initial strut placed between the two stern plates for support. You can see how it fits with the six other deck plates.

Don't be in too much of a hurry to get the top deck laid. We like to leave these pieces for last because you never know when you may have to get in back of one of the side plates for one reason or another—usually because it has slipped out of place and needs a little push—and if you close the ship up you

Fig. 18-16 The gun ports, edges evened with foil. The line of the hull has been partly beaded.

214

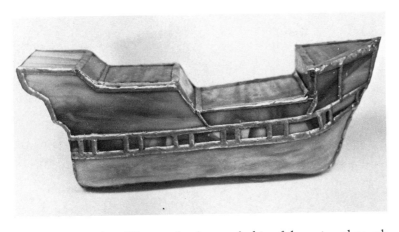

Fig. 18-17 The completed
frame of the ship. All surfaces
have been beaded.

can't manage this. Things also have a habit of dropping through
those little ports and not coming out again. Drips of solder are especially irritating in this regard. It's easier to reach in and pick
them out than try to shake them out—and a lot safer.

It doesn't matter in what arrangement you place your deck
plates; the last one will always be the most difficult because you
can't get behind it. It's a good idea to make your last piece one
of the smaller plates, one of the strut walls, perhaps, so you can
maneuver it more easily; make sure it fits snugly before you start
to solder. Work carefully because if it drops through into the
hull, you'll have to tear up a portion of deck to get it out.

When you have everything neat and to your satisfaction, you
have completed the first stage of the project.

THE MASTS AND DECK FURNITURE

*The Temporary Stand*

Up to now we have been working on the body of the ship,
turning it in almost every position to accomplish the soldering.
From here we are going to be working topside and we must have
the ship upright. Nothing fancy; a piece of copper sheeting will
do for the stand if it is wide enough. Clean off a portion of the
copper so it will accept solder, and run some beads of solder
along the lower joint of the hull to the copper. This will stand
the ship up and still allow you to turn it to either side (see Figure 18-18).

We want to add enough material to the decks so we will have a
nautical feeling. We don't want to get so carried away that we
end up with a garbage scow. Our first step, therefore, is to check
perspective. First we'll put up some railing; this will give us a size
which will provide a measure for other items.

*The Railing*

Four posts are involved on each side of the prow; three on
each side of the stern. These are heavy ¾" high pieces of copper

215

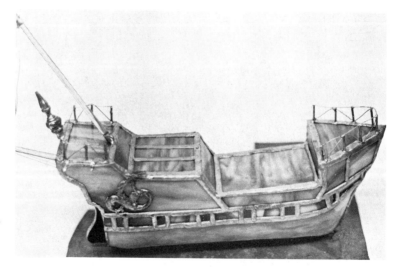

Fig. 18-18 The temporary stand, the railing, the first mast, the sternspar and the rudder. Note the two strips of copper foil along the middle deck.

wire which are tinned and soldered into the border foil of the deck at calculated intervals. A thinner wire is strung along the tops of these posts and soldered to them. This same wire is strung alternately from top to bottom to provide a fence (see Fig. 18-18). You have to solder pretty carefully at the bottom joints so as not to knock the posts loose; a quick dab should do it.

*The Stern Plate Design*

Looking over our railing at the wide expanse of stern plate, we felt something more was needed. We settled on a brass design cut from a wide piece of lamp banding which not only fit just right but added the proper amount of golden sparkle to either side. This piece is soldered into the upper and lower foil lines as seen in Figure 18-18.

*The Stern Figurehead*

Many old sailing ships had an ornate afterpiece at the taffrail; ours, continuing in the lamp milieu, is a brass lamp finial. We wrapped copper foil around its lower portion since this brass could not be soldered. We also laid a strip of brass banding across the back of the stern deck to support this backward leaning device, since the foil alone would tend to pull away with the weight. To the front and back (fore and aft) of this finial, we decided to place our first two masts (see Fig. 18-18).

*The Mizzenmast*

This is in front of the stern figurehead angled in the same direction (see Figs. 18-18 and 18-19). In reality it's a glass stirring rod pressed into service (like the crew, possibly) and is solid. It is 6″ tall and we prepared it for fastening to the deck in the same fashion as the stern figurehead: by wrapping copper foil

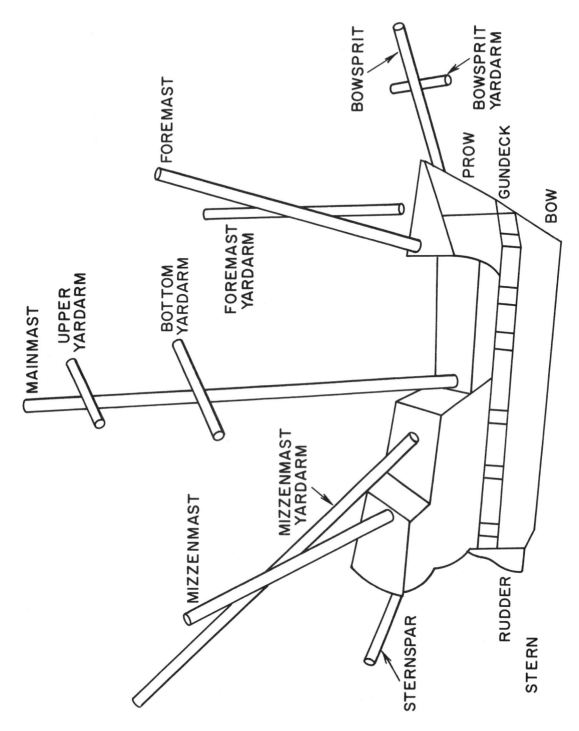

Fig. 18-19  Ship with masts and parts labeled.

217

round its bottom and soldering this closed. We already had a convenient seam to solder to and the mast was easily raised. We placed another roll of foil round the top of the mast. It is not necessary to use solid glass rods for these masts; we alternated them with glass tubing cut to measure, just to show it all looks the same.

### The Sternspar

This is the back rod sticking out over the water (see Figs. 18-18 and 18-19). It is an important addition because just as the mizzenmast gives us a beginning conception of height, this mast provides us with a taste of elongation. Our sense of design is no longer limited to the boat proper now and we can get a freer notion of the space we intend to fill. This will come into sharper focus as we continue to get the masts and rigging in position and will culminate in our placement of the air itself—via the sails.

The sternspar is a short 2½″ rod, and is angled slightly upward from its attachment to the back of the upper deck (see Figs. 18-18 and 18-19). As with the description of the mast above, copper foil is wrapped around both ends. Just to get an idea how the rigging was going to look we ran the first strands of representative wire from the mizzenmast to the sternspar and from the sternspar to the ship. We will have more to say about the rigging shortly. As long as we are at this end of the ship, it might be good to mention the rudder.

### The Rudder

You can see the rudder peeking out the back of the ship in Figures 18-19 and 18-20. It's attached to the upper and lower solder lines of the hull. We cut the rudder out of two pieces of black glass double glazed; one piece looked scarcely powerful enough to maneuver a ship of this size.

### The Central Zone of the Decks

Each deck with the exception of the prow deck will have an object in its center. The stern deck will have the wheel and binnacle, the middle deck will have the cabin and the lower deck will show the opening to the fo'castle. Each of these objects must be attached firmly to areas where there are no seams to solder to. How do we get around this? Figure 18-18 shows one way: by extending tinned copper tape over the surface of the middle deck as a soldering area. This is inoffensive only if enough of these tracks will be covered by the object in mind. The other alternative is to glue the object to the deck using Duco cement, and we have done this as well for purposes of demonstrating both techniques. Often, in constructing sculptured pieces, you need them both.

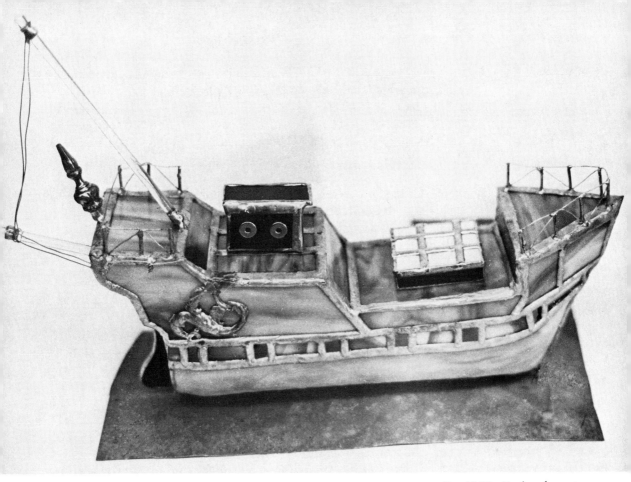

Fig. 18-20 Further elements are added: the cabin (left) and the forecastle (right).

*The Cabin and the Forecastle* Figure 18-21 demonstrates the construction of these items. The cabin on the left is 1½″ high by 2″ long and ½″ wide. We made it of black glass foiled all around. The portholes are steel washers glued into place.

The forecastle is really a skylight and we did our best to make it look like one. Black glass borders ¼″ high are overlayed by white, semitransparent glass. Our old favorite flashed white opal

Fig. 18-21 The cabin and forecastle seen close up.

can be used to good effect. Width is 2″ and length approximately the same. After the piece has been foiled together around the edges, ³/₁₆″ copper tape is run across the top in checkerboard pattern and soldered to the borders and beaded. This gives the effect of panes of glass.

Figure 18-20 shows the boat with both the above described items in place; the one soldered, the other foiled. The forecastle is placed not in the exact center of its deck but, in order to leave plenty of room for the mainmast, closer to the prow.

*The Wheel and Binnacle*　We show in Figure 18-22 how these items appear by themselves. You can get some idea of the size of the complex by the fingers holding them. The wheel is a brass circle, a lamp spacer will do, to which are soldered the spokes, small pieces of brass tubing which have been crimped at their un-soldered ends.

The binnacle is the top of a test tube cut on a bias with the long end facing the front of the ship. This will give it its proper backward tilt. This tilt should not be exaggerated; a minimal leaning sternside is all that's required. Into the closed end of the test tube, we pushed a piece of paper with some ink markings to give the appearance of a compass. The wheel is attached to the binnacle by a piece of copper tape wrapped round the top of the tube and tinned; this furnishes a soldering surface.

The binnacle is attached to the ship by applying a roll of copper

Fig. 18-22　The wheel and binnacle.

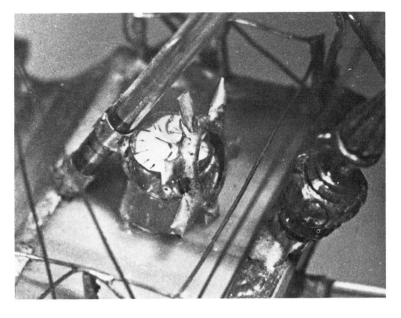

Fig. 18-23   The wheel and binnacle in proper position on deck.

tape at a corresponding level of the mizzenmast and soldering the two items together (see Fig. 18-23).

*The Ropes*   Atop the cabin and the forecastle are coiled extra lines (see Fig. 18-24). Their presence gives a sense of life aboard. These are not a result of twisting wire just any which way; they have to *look* like rope. We had to practice a bit and found the most natural effect was achieved by using two separate strands of wire and scrambling them together.

Fig. 18-24   The zones of the deck seen close up.

An end or a loop of this wire, whichever seems easier, is soldered to one of the lead lines; in the cabin this will be necessarily one of the border leads. Do not get too much solder on the wire; it detracts from the rope-like look. These little touches, done to perfection, will be what makes your end result so spectacular. Some viewers find the rope one of the most effective presentations on the ship.

### Foremast and Mainmast

The foremast, the one most toward the front, is made from another stirrer (see Fig. 18-19). It is longer than the mizzenmast, measuring about 8″, and is placed slanting a bit foreward. Follow the same procedures for attaching it to the deck as you did for the mizzenmast.

The mainmast, which you can see the bottom portion in Figure 18-24, is the first mast we have used that is a colored glass rod and is of considerable thickness. Despite this fact, it is cut to size the same as the thinner rods—with a glasscutter. Instead of one nick, you have to make small cuts all along the circumference until you get completely around. The rod can then be snapped with the hands like flat glass. It may be necessary to smooth the bottom of such a thick rod with Carborundum paper so it will be absolutely flat against the deck.

### The Dory

Alongside the cabin we have fabricated a small boat out of a piece of sheet copper. This dory is placed carelessly against the cabin, one edge upward, and is soldered to the bottom track on the deck (see Fig. 18-24). It makes an effective small touch.

You can make it fairly quickly from a flat piece of copper by drawing the bottom shape as a triangle with bowed sides. Fold these sides up while maintaining the flat bottom. Pinch the front edges together and solder them. This prow will be the first holding joint. Then fold up the back edge; you must cut down from the sides with shears to do this or else you will kink the side folds. You will be left with some excess back here; cut it away, solder the back to the upright side seams and you have a dandy dory.

### The Crow's Nest and the First Two Yardarms

In Figure 18-25, we see a full view of the project thus far. Note how the masts, especially the mainmast, have augmented our original design, providing an outflung complexion to the clustered ship. Part of the fun in working with this project is to see how it extends and varies with every added piece.

Despite the reach of the mainmast, a good 13″, it is well supported by the single solder joint at its foot. Now at the first level,

Fig. 18-25 The ship so far showing the mainmast with its yardarms and the foremast. The crow's nest is seen between the yardarms.

8″ from the lower deck, we place upon the mainmast the bottom yardarm. This is either a stirrer or a glass rod cut to a 6½″ length and attached with the usual copper foil wrap. At 11″ from the deck, the upper 5″ yardarm is soldered. Between the two, about 9½″ from the deck, is the crow's nest—a small platform which circles the mast and provides certain problems of its own in cutting.

In Figure 18-26, we see how the crow's nest must be cut. The major difficulty is getting out the fairly deep (for such a small piece of glass) inner curve. The trick here, as shown in the top piece, is to cut the inner curve before trying to cut the upper arm. If you cut that thin upper arm and then try to get the curve out, the strain from the middle of the indentation comes forward against the arms and one of them, usually the thinner, is likely to snap. Both pieces of the crow's nest are exactly alike; one being the mirror image of the other. They are foiled into place just like the yardarms.

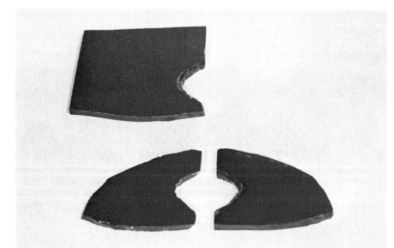

Fig. 18-26 The crow's nest close up.

Fig. 18-27 Making the ladder.

There are two ladders, one to each side, and they should be exactly alike. They are 1½″ wide at the base, about ¼″ up top and stretch for a length of 8″. They will reach from the ladder extensions of the deck to attach to the mainmast directly below the crow's nest. In Figure 18-27, we see how the ladder is fabricated. It is a time-consuming job, but don't skimp on any of the rungs. Two types of wire are used: heavy wire the size of the deck posts and a thinner wire similar to the one used for the deck fencing. This is the wire that will also be used for the rigging.

The first step in making the ladder is to cut four strands (make sure they are straight) of the heavy wire. Solder them together at the top with two on the outside and two on the inside of a very small triangle. If you tried to solder them all together, the top of the ladder would be too bulky. Now the two inner strands will be longer than the outer ones; even them all up with a shears. Spread the feet of the ladder to the requisite distance and solder in the first rung.

There's a lot of copper to solder here; don't try to hold it with your fingers or you'll burn them. In Figure 18-27, you can see how we clamped the upper portion of the ladder to a tabletop and let the rest of it stick out over the table. Now it is supported and we can work on it with both hands.

We did not measure and cut small strands of wire for the rungs; we worked with one long strand of wire and soldered and cut as we progressed. You need not measure the distance between the respective rungs; an eye measurement is adequate.

Be sure to flux well at every joint or the solder won't take. Don't use so much solder that you plug up the rungs; this looks horribly sloppy and makes your ladder quite impractical. Don't worry about the little nibs of wire that will be left along the side of the ladder as you snip the wire away after each rung is soldered. When the ladder is completed, you can use a grinding wheel or a file to smooth out this surface. Remember to do it however. It's a small point, but again this whole project sinks or floats on small points.

Once your ladders are completed, attach them to the ship as shown in Figure 18-28. Do not attach them to the deck proper; instead add a ladder extension. These extensions are pieces of glass, one on each side, which measure ½″ wide by 2″ long. We cut them out of black glass and soldered them to the middle deck along the outside lead line so they actually hang over the water. The ladder feet are then soldered to the outside lead line of these extensions. This provides a more pleasing line to the ship and allows less crowding on the middle deck. It also gives a nicer angle to the ladders against the mast.

Fig. 18-28 About half the
rigging in place.

### The Mizzenmast and Foremast Yardarms

Figure 18-28 shows the angles at which these yardarms are placed (also see Fig. 18-19). We have slanted them this way because of the manner in which we want the sails that will be attached to them to catch the wind. The mizzenmast yardarm is the longest on the ship; it measures 10″ and must be supported by more than the mizzenmast itself. Fortunately the ladder is conveniently at hand and the end of this tubing, wrapped in foil, is soldered to the ladder. We are going to be soldering to a lot of the rigging as well to support various elements, as you will see. The foremast yardarm is smaller, measuring 6″, and can take its angle supported by its mast alone. This angle is about the same as that of the mizzenmast yardarm seen from the front.

### The Bowsprit

The bowsprit is the long rod coming out of the prow which we see in Figure 18-28 for the first time (also see Fig. 18-19). We used the same width rod as for the mainmast and sanded the front round with Carborundum paper as we did for the top of the mainmast. These two rods provide the most forceful masts on the ship and we felt they should have more of a finished quality.

The bowsprit measures 4½″ and comes up from just beneath the prow at an angle of about 120° with the front line of the ship.

226

It is the final long extension of the original design and completes the ship's basic silhouette. Beneath the bowsprit, 3″ from the front of the ship to which it is soldered, we place the bowsprit yardarm; the last to go on. It is a glass tube the width of all the others but by far the smallest, measuring only 3¼″.

*The Bow Figurehead*

We were at some pains to decide what to do here. We finally decided on a metal figurehead rather than glass for several reasons. First, it would complement the stern figurehead; second, a glass figurehead would take up too much width and disturb the line of the ship. We settled on a copper stamping from among our collection of such. (Always purchase these little odds and ends when you get a chance; they're inexpensive, you never know when they will come in handy and they're always impossible to find when you desperately need one. Hobby stores are good places to look.) We were fortunate enough to locate a copper seahorse which we promptly soldered into place (see Fig. 18-29). Do this carefully so as not to get excess solder over the

Fig. 18-29   The ship with its sails and the final brass rod stand.

copper—it won't come off and you may end up having to tin the whole surface. On either side of the head of this figure, we glued a millefiore which gave it a truly formidable pair of eyes and added just the right amount of color to what otherwise might be too much an expanse of metal.

*The Cannons and Hatch Covers*

The cannons are ½″ pieces of ⅛″ wide hollow brass tubing. You have to cut these pieces with a hacksaw so as not to crimp the ends. They are soldered into the gun ports at the stern angle of each with about ⅜″ of the tube sticking out. Don't smear solder all over the tube; a little dab at the corner will hold it tight. The back two cannons should be pointed slightly to the stern; the remaining four take a bearing more and more toward the bow, following the line of the ship.

Above each cannon is a hatch cover, ostensibly hinged and lashed to the gun deck at about a 120° angle (see Fig. 18-29). You must use very flat pieces of copper about ½″ wide by ⅜″ long for these covers and, again, we want them to show as much copper as possible so don't oversolder.

## THE RIGGING AND THE SAILS

These items must be considered together because they have to go into place together. Some of the rigging is dependent on the position of a sail; some of the sails must have the rigging present for support.

The rigging is all copper wire and we saw an example of how it is placed in a previous figure. It is not enough merely to run single strands of copper wire haphazardly; they must look realistic. Accordingly, we will be running in some instances double and triple strands to indicate pulley systems; we will even indicate the pulleys. This is all part of that same attention to detail which makes this project seaworthy. Refer to Figures 18-19, 18-28, and 18-29 as you work.

*The Pulleys*

We first thought of using the heads of push pins for pulleys but they were out of proportion. We located a nail the head of which had an indentation suitable for coiling wire. Minus the nail part, this proved satisfactory and as you go through the latter figures of this project you will see pulleys hanging hither and yon throughout the rigging. Pulleys hang from one strand of wire and invariably have at least two, sometimes three or four, strands of wire coming from them. Watch for the pulleys in the photographs as we proceed and try to place yours the same way.

*The Mizzenmast Rigging*

Two wires go from the top of the mizzenmast to the back of the sternspar. From here two wires go to either side of the stern, about ½″ from its back line, where we have soldered small pieces of heavy wire jutting out to take these lines. From these jutting wires at the sides (they are about ¼″ long and we will refer to them as cleats), two wires on either side travel upward to the top of the mizzenmast. That makes for quite a few wires traveling to the top of this mast; you can solder them or better still wind them round the top. From the stern portion of the mizzenmast yardarm, a pulley hangs about 1″ down supported by one wire; from the pulley three wires hang to wrap around the back of the sternspar.

*The Mizzenmast Sail*

We made a double bent copper form, triangular in shape and not quite as long as the mizzenmast yardarm, and fit it in place, making sure it hung well above the deck. Using the same technique as for making the hull, we cast a piece of flashed white opal glass to this shape, foiled it and attached it to the mizzenmast yardarm (see Fig. 18-29). Along the length of yardarm to be used, we wrapped spaced coils of copper foil. These give the appearance of sail rings and are, of course, in reality soldering points.

The part of this sail that hangs over the stern is supported by and soldered to those wires with which it naturally comes in contact. Here's a good example of decor being functional as well as realistic. Along the open area of yardarm, we placed a small flat piece of glass; this represents part of the sail still furled to the mast.

*The Mainmast Rigging*

We'll start from the top and work down. A single wire stretches from ½″ below the top of this mast where it is wound to each end of the top yardarm. Another single wire goes from the juncture of yardarm and mast to either end of the crow's nest. From this same area of the mast, two other long single wires stretch down to the ship's sides to cleats about 1″ foreward of the cleats previously described.

From the ends of the top mainmast yardarm, wires stretch as follows: (1) two single wires to either side run parallel to the ends of the yardarm below; (2) a single wire runs to a pulley; from here two wires run to the top of the mizzenmast; a single wire runs to the back stern cleat. This wiring must be duplicated on the other side.

From the center of the mainmast at the level of the top yardarm, a single wire runs to the top of the mizzenmast and then to the end of the mizzenmast yardarm (you can solder it down to one of the sail rings).

From the center of the mainmast, a single wire runs to either side from the level of the lower mainmast yardarm to a cleat soldered to a point where the middle plate top line meets the back plate. We'll label this the central cleat.

### The Mainmast Sails

The two mainmast sails are now placed. These are C-shaped with a large inner curve cut from the bottom, larger sail to allow it to fit into the mast. They are attached to the yardarms as previously described and are also supported by and soldered to those wires which they naturally fall against. In the case of the lower sail, this will be the lines going to the central cleat; in the case of the upper sail, the supporting wire is the forward of the two going to the ends of the yardarms.

### The Foremast Rigging

Two discrete wires run parallel from the top of the foremast to the end of the bowsprit where they are soldered to the familiar copper coil.

A single line goes from the top of the foremast to the upper end of the foremast yardarm. Another goes to either end of the lower mainmast yardarm. Still another travels to the upper portion of the mainmast just above the upper yardarm and the last, from this position, goes to the left (with the ship facing you) end of the upper mainmast yardarm.

From the upper end of the foremast yardarm, a pulley is extended horizontal to the deck; from here a wire goes to the right end of the upper mainmast yardarm and another to the same portion of the lower mainmast yardarm and two more to the central cleat. These same wires run on the other side with the exception of a wire to the upper yardarm.

From the central portion of the foremast, where it holds the yardarm, two wires run, on either side, to cleats placed at the back prow plate upper line one in front of the other. These are the foreward cleats. These lines just described run over the ship's railing as do all lines; never through it.

### The Foremast Sail

This sail is an S curve like the mizzenmast sail, but blunter and not as wide. We have swung its free end over the water, following the line laid down by the slant of its yardarm. The bottom portion of this sail must just clear the railing.

230

*The Bowsprit Rigging*

Two parallel wires travel from the end of the bowsprit to either end of its yardarm. Above the attachment of its yardarm, two discrete wires travel on either side to the foreward first cleat. From the yardarm attachment itself, two wires run to the prow centerline and attach almost at the bottom of the hull. From the ends of the bowsprit yardarm, two wires go to the second foreward cleat and two to the prow, meeting those from the center and other side.

*The Flying Jib*

This is the little sail under the bowsprit. It looks like a miniature of the lower mainsail. Its lower end goes backward and upward supported by and soldered to the lower bowsprit yardarm prow lines. Leave enough of a curvature in the center when cutting the glass so as not to run into the prow figurehead.

*The Fore-Skysail*

This is the front sail. It is the least bent of all the sails, but it serves the purpose intended: to show the wind gathering force. In another moment it will fill. This is the only sail not soldered to a mast; it is soldered directly to the foremast-bowsprit rigging which holds it quite securely.

*The Sail Stays*

All the sails have lines running from their ends to points that are meaningful. The fore-skysail stay is a wire going from the point of the sail to the center cleat. The lower mainsail stays also go, on either side, to this cleat. The mizzensail stay goes to the end of the stern spar. All other sail stays are combined automatically in the rigging described for their areas.

A note about the rigging. As we mentioned, all these wires should appear purposeful; they should therefore be as taut as possible and take natural gravitational curves where necessary. You had best use a vise to pull the wrinkles and loops out of the wire; to attempt to straighten them once they're soldered into position is hopeless.

FINISHING TOUCHES

We added a bell on the stern deck; the ship called for one and we located one readily enough in the "findings" section of a hobby shop. We also placed a pennant on the top of the mast; you can use a straight piece of glass here; we preferred to bend our pennant a bit so it ripples in the wind. We added another cannon to the lower deck across from the mainmast; a small piece of brass tubing and two small earring findings for the wheels did the job. Along each open side of the lower deck we laid ⅛″ wide hollow brass tubing to emphasize and raise the line of the ship at this level. The final finishing touches we saved for the bow.

*Ornamenting the Bow*

All of this has to do with the anchor. First we placed the hawse-hole—the anchor chain compartment. There is no necessity to make an actual hole; indicating it will do. We used a ½″ wide, brass lamp ring and, placing it at the bottom juncture of the first prow plate, soldered it to the lead lines available. Once more, as in other areas, use a dab of solder only; we want to preserve the brass color.

For the anchor chain, you must be guided in size by the hawse-hole; it should look as though the chain would be effective to hold the ship and not be too large or small to fit reasonably in its compartment. Use brass chain; solder one end to the ring and let it hang down about 1½″; then loop it up and over some of the outside wires coming from the bowsprit complex and solder it to them. Continue it from here to the juncture of the second prow plate and middle plate and solder the end of the chain to this section.

As for anchors, you can acquire small anchors if you wish; we made ours from two fish hooks with the eyes cut off and held together on top by a copper foil wrap. We soldered this top area to the upper line of the middle prow plate; this holds the anchor tight against the side of the ship. Large plastic or glass beads held with wire and soldered to masts and rigging give the impression of free-swinging lanterns.

## THE STAND AND THE OCEAN

*The Stand*

The ship itself is completed at this point. However, continuing with our purpose to make it as realistic and colorful as possible, we need a sturdy stand that will hold it upright while at the same time will not interfere with the shape we have so carefully developed.

The only way this can be accomplished is to hold the ship from the bottom as we have been doing with the copper. We substitute for the copper three brass rods soldered in a Z shape (see Fig. 18-29). The back of the ship rests on the top horizontal bar of the Z and the prow sits on the front one. The diagonal bar forming the center of the Z supports the two ends and the middle of the ship as it crosses beneath. The bottom of the ship is soldered securely to these points from the hull seam. You have to do this with the ship upright but it isn't difficult.

232

The Sailboat

The Spider Window

The Mercedes Window

The Birdhouse

Mirror with Stained Glass Frame

The Townhouse Terrarium

The Menorah

The Painted Ship

The Trellis

Coat of Arms

The Sunflower

The Triple Glazed Bird

The Fierce Fish

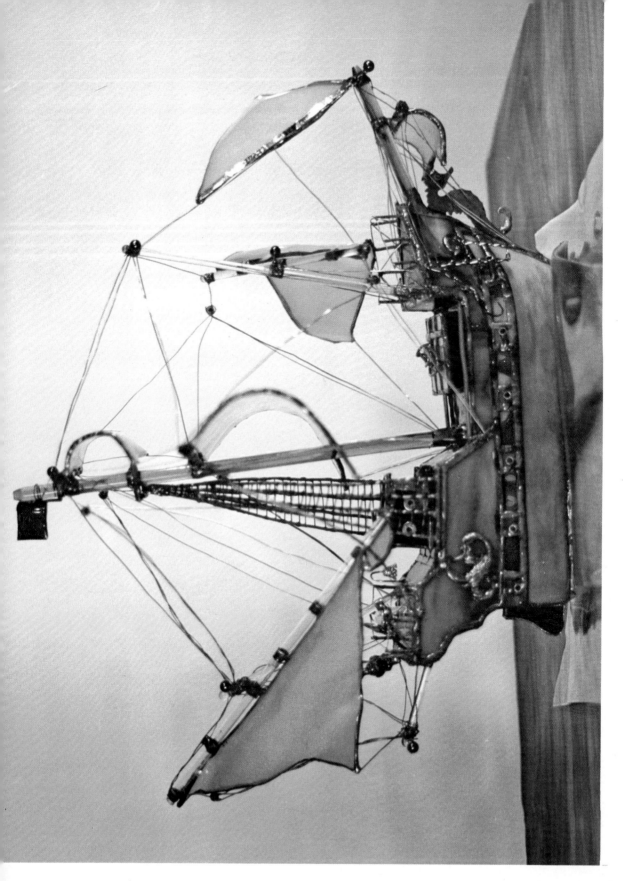

Glass Galleon

Fig. 18-30 The completed
Glass Galleon gliding
through the waves. (See
color section)

However, this will not support the ship completely, topheavy
as it is with masts and rigging and sails. We therefore add two
supporting bars on one side. Make your mind up which side of
your ship will be facing you and add these bars on the other side.
We used heavy, tinned copper wire and soldered the ends below
to the brass piping and above to the top line of the hull. With
these bars in place, your ship is tip-proof in the stormiest sea—as
you will soon discover.

### The Ocean and Waves

Get a piece of blue and white opalescent glass at least three
times the width and length of your ship. Cut it in a square or rectangular shape if you wish (we did) or leave it irregular, providing it shows curved, not angled, edges.

Using the same technique as previously for the sails and hull,
bend other pieces of the glass to look like waves against the ship's
side (see Fig. 18-30). These waves will accomplish two purposes:

233

they will enhance the apparent motion of the vessel and they will hide that portion of the stand facing you so your ship will appear to be cruising through the water on its own.

Now all you have to do is lay your flat piece of glass on an appropriate table, put your ship on top of it with the proper side outward, put the waves in place against it and you have a unique and provocative display.

# IN CONCLUSION

Well, you've gotten this far so you've completed everything and your house is well decorated. By now you are prepared for the standard question: "How long did it take you to make that?" No doubt the pyramid builders were plagued with the identical query. So . . . in reply to *your* interrogation, we'll tell you how long it took us to make them—approximately.

The Birdhouse—1 hour
The Townhouse Terrarium—4 hours
The Sailboat—3 hours
The Triple Glazed Bird—8 hours
The Menorah—4 hours
The Smiling Monk—3 hours for the prototype; after that 3 minutes
Coat of Arms—24 hours
The Sunflower—24 hours
Glass Galleon—60 hours
The Lightbox—2 hours

Of course the question should be: How much enjoyment did you get from them? Our answer: immeasurable.

We hope your answer's the same.

# Part 3

# APPENDIX

# MAKING
# A LIGHTBOX

There may be minimal window space in a home; wall space, however, is not at such a premium. Stained glass can utilize wall areas just as paintings do. The only difference is stained glass must be backlighted to be effective; hence a lightbox. This object need not be bulky and should not be aesthetically objectionable; it should meld with the other furniture in the room. If more than one lightbox is to be exhibited in the same room, they should be uniform in choice of wood, staining and molding. The result can be a striking display not only of your work in stained glass but your decorative ability.

THE WOODEN SHAPE

We have made circular lightboxes to complement such stained glass windows but we feel this is the province of the carpenter. Anyone can make a square lightbox, however; and even if you have an oval window, it can be fitted to a square box by blocking out the corners with properly shaped pieces of wood. Museums exhibit stained glass in this fashion.

So you are going to have four sides and a back. Steps to be considered are: (1) mitering the corners; (2) calculating the depth for the bulbs; (3) routing (rabbeting) the presenting edges; and (4) changing bulbs.

Figure A-1 shows a typical lightbox with the front portion removed. All the above criteria have been satisfied.

MITERING THE CORNERS

A miter box will help; use a metal one so you won't cut into it. Mitering gives your box a professionally finished look which will be transmitted to your panel. It also adds to the strength of the box. Use fairly thick wood which will allow mitering and rab-

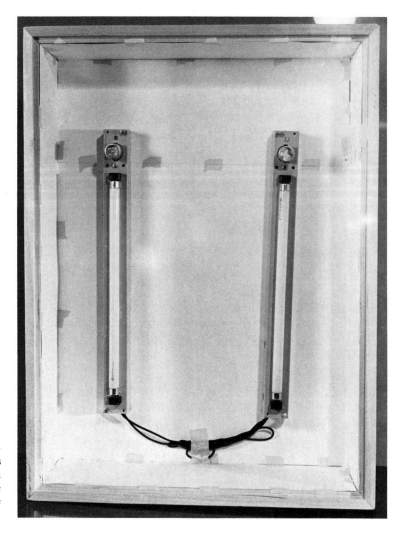

Fig. A-1 Inside the light-box. The small fluorescents are spaced apart and extra cord is taped down. The wood is lined with white paper.

beting. We use birch (a good, inexpensive cabinet wood) almost an inch thick.

CALCULATING THE BULB DEPTH

Always use fluorescent bulbs; daylight fluorescents give the truest illumination. Regular light bulbs tend to leave "hot spots" no matter how you try to soften them. They also give a yellow glow. Old light boxes had special side tiers built to permit this type of bulb to be used alongside, rather than under, the glass. That's hardly necessary today. Fluorescents require placement about six inches away from the overlying panel; this is still a comfortable outcropping from the wall as a heavily framed paint-ing may take almost that much. Our side pieces for the lightbox shown here measure exactly 6″, including the molding.

240

Routing can be done by a carpenter who already has the tools handy. To do it yourself will require use of a router or tablesaw. You shouldn't attempt to do this freehand.

The depth of this routed shelf depends on the thickness of your border glass plus the lead plus the underlying glass or plastic used to spread the flow of light. All of this should come even with the surface of the wood to permit your molding to lie flat. Machine made glass is generally ⅛" thick, add two surfaces of lead came with a U back as another ⅛" and underlying diffusing material as yet another similar fraction and ⅜" should be your proper depth. If you are using antique glass where thickness is variable, you'll have to take the thickest measurement and conform to that. If the thickness is all to one side, compensate accordingly in the depth of the wood on that side.

The width of the routed shelf depends on how much or little border lead you want showing as well as how much support you think is necessary for the weight of the panel. Some individuals take the wood right up to the glass; others prefer a narrow lead border. Whatever you decide, make sure it's the same on all edges. It's not a bad idea to get this part of your lightbox done professionally. It's easy to slip a little bit and end up with a routed area that's crooked in either depth or width. Then your panel will lie crooked.

You may find a problem once the routing is done in that your panel won't quite fit. Don't try to force it; the likelihood is that your border leads are slightly bowed or a solder joint is bulging. Try to accommodate the panel to the wood even if you have to un-solder and re-solder border leads. Of course if this becomes an extensive project you'd better recheck your measurements; you may have to re-route the wood. Ideally the panel should fit within the routed sections with a small amount of play to allow for expansion of the glass with changes in temperature.

CHANGING BULBS

It's amazing how many people forget this will have to be done. If you lock your lightbox up tighter than Fort Knox, you'll get only a one time use out of it. Changing bulbs can be accomplished through either front or back. Coming through the back is probably the easiest method. Rather than nailing the back in place against the sides use four screws with flat heads. These are easily undone when necessary and the bulbs can be changed. In this case, don't tape your inside reflective material from sides to back or you'll pull it away and will end up having to take the whole box apart to fix it.

The front approach is more of a nuisance but some prefer it. It involves prying the molding away and lifting out the panel and bottom plate. Never try to accomplish this with the lightbox hanging on the wall—even though this is why some prefer the front approach. You will unbalance it and likely break something.

REFLECTIVE MATERIAL

In Figure A-1, you see the inside of the box has been covered with white paper taped into place. You can use tinfoil if you prefer. We find it harder to work with and no more reflective. It also tends to tear readily and invariably creases. Whatever reflective material you decide on, cover all inner surfaces, permitting the light to splash around the box freely. Some workers insist on gluing this material to the wood; this takes longer and adds nothing to the final effect. You won't see the tape through the front.

PLACEMENT OF THE LIGHTS

The lights should be placed equally apart, centered and held firmly to the back of the box by screws. The size of the box determines the size and number of lights. In a large box, consider placing lights horizontally as well as vertically. However, it is rarely necessary in the usual home lightbox to go this far. If anything, excessive lighting is usually time and money consuming. Lights that are placed closer together than 6″ are wasted. Don't be fooled by turning on your fluorescents prior to placing your light spreading medium and thinking the incandescence is inadequate.

The electric cords should be combined into one and lead through a hole in the bottom (occasionally in the top) of the box. A line switch affixed at the proper level will complete the electrical work.

Everything inside the box must be firmly held in place. Extra wire is taped down. You don't want things jumping about inside when you hang your box for display.

THE LIGHT SPREADING MEDIUM

Figure A-2 displays the lightbox ready for the panel. The bulbs are lit and there is an even flow of light over the front plate. Such a plate is necessary to spread the light. The best fluorescents will not throw illumination prerequisite to the needs of stained glass by themselves; you will see "hot spots"—areas of sharp incandescence around the bulbs. There are two types of material that work well for spreading light: glass and plastic.

Fig. A-2 The backing of white flashed opal glass spreads the light evenly.

*Plastic*

White opaque plastic works satisfactorily, but is difficult to come by. You'll end up having to purchase a large sheet and whacking off a hunk that fits your particular box. This isn't easy, especially if you aren't used to working with plastic and do not have the proper tools. We've tried cutting the stuff with a coping saw and a hacksaw. Aside from the arm of the saw eventually interfering with the cut, the dust raised is ferocious. Plastic tends to fragment while it is being cut and you'll have a lot of waste. The Fletcher-Terry Company manufactures a cutter especially for plastic (see Sources of Supply). If you are going to do any amount of work with this material, get one.

Aside from its cutting difficulties, plastic scratches readily;

243

Fig. A-3 The completed panel on the lightbox. The lights are on.

these scratches retain dust and dirt which appear as fine lines that can be visible through your panel. And it's no cheaper than glass—especially since you can purchase a smaller quantity of the latter for the same amount of use.

*Ground Glass*

Even the most highly ground glass is disappointing in this respect. It's expensive and only partially masks the bulbs below. Don't waste your money.

*Flashed White Opaque Glass*

This is unquestionably our favorite. It is easy to cut, easy to fit, comes in thicknesses of ⅛″, cleans well and spreads light as evenly and more crisply than plastic. It is readily available— most commercial glass shops stock it—and you can have it cut to any size you wish. Don't confuse it with opalescent white which is

244

a solid color. Flashed glass is colored on the surfaces and traps the light within it, diffusing it like neon.

THE PANEL IN PLACE

It is not necessary to fasten the illuminating plate to the lightbox; the stained glass panel will keep it in place. In Figure A-3, we see the completed project. Molding has been nailed around the outside edges from which a moderate portion of lead border peeks. Use small brads here; four to a side will do. And use a tack hammer. If you overdo the pounding when nailing your molding, you may find yourself with a number of free-form cracks in the glass. We placed brads in each corner and two along the sides. Raise the lightbox on end and check its stability. All that remains is to run picture wire behind it and hang it on the wall.

# PHOTOGRAPHING STAINED GLASS

Don't shoot yourself when something goes astray with an enterprise; shoot a picture. That is also true for successful endeavors, but it can be just as important to know why something didn't work out. At some future date, you may want to re-evaluate this particular failure; only photographs will enable you to do so.

There are other reasons for keeping a camera handy in the studio. If you intend to make items for sale, or sell yourself as an instructor or a craftsman, you must have a portfolio. For your information as well as any prospective client's, you must keep your imagination on file. A customer can get the best idea of your capacities and you can observe what your development has been. Many projects you might like to describe or remember may have already been sold; in these cases, your only record is what you have on film. We learned this the hard way and eventually had to make pilgrimmages to homes far and wide to get pictures of long ago purchased items. And then, you never know when you might want to do a magazine article on some special technique; sequential photographs are a must.

WHAT KIND OF CAMERA?

A 35 millimeter is good for off the shoulder as well as posed shots. However an Instamatic® can do the job if you are just starting. We use a Pentax® and a Rolliflex®. The larger Rolliflex negative gives sharper enlargements than the smaller camera and we like the softness of the lens.

A lot depends on how much photography you plan to do. Start off with whatever camera you have on hand. Remember, the object is to make a photographic record, not to become a professional photographer. As you do more and more work, and more and more pictures seem to be demanded, you may get into the camera scene so deep it becomes a hobby on its own. At that

246

point, you may have two or more cameras, and you'll probably begin developing your own film and making your own prints.

## LIGHTING

How you illuminate your subject matter is critical. Poor lighting can make the loveliest item resemble a witch's tooth, while on the other hand lighting that enhances the glass will give authority to a merely so-so work. Many professional photographers have never shot stained glass so you can't always rely on them to do justice to your pieces. Even if a professional does the camera work, you may have to arrange the lighting yourself.

Correct lighting depends on the glass involved. Transparent glass must be backlit to gain any photographic vivacity. Proper backlighting depends on an even flow of illumination and avoiding hot spots from the bulbs. White plastic sheeting or flashed white opal glass must be used as a screen for this purpose. Strobe lighting is generally ineffectual from behind unless such a screen is used, and even with a screen is unsatisfactory for larger panels because the light spread is uneven.

Even with proper positioning, an overabundance of light solely from the rear presents the camera with such stark lines for the leading that the print resembles a cartoon. This effect is not apparent to your eyes which have a built in depth of field. To enable the camera to give depth to the leading, these areas must be highlighted from the front. Cross lighting works best; bulbs of the same intensity should be used from right and left and the lamps evenly spaced to avoid shadowing. All front lighting should throw a wide enough illumination to completely wash the object; avoid pin spots. The tendency is to use the front lights for emphasis; such lighting may reflect back into the lens and will come out on the print as a dazzling blur.

Painted pieces that contain matted background can forego being lit from the front since the matt diffuses the background lighting pretty well within the glass. Even the leading will show highlights from behind; it is your choice whether to emphasize this by throwing some light from the front as well. You might try it both ways and pick the finished print you like best.

Opalescent glass is mostly front lit though background lighting can emphasize the pattern of such glasses. If we backlight an opalescent piece, we also take the shot reflected solely from the front and choose the most effective view from the print. You can't tell from eyesight alone.

The thing to bear in mind is that the camera lens does not see exactly what you see. It has its own perspectives and none of your emotions regarding your work. From this standpoint alone, it's worth having your camera handy.

## COLOR

Slides, we find, are better than prints because they are more versatile. You can show them on a one-to-one basis either in a small viewer or just by holding them up to the light; you can project them; you can have them reproduced through color separations; and if you end up wanting a print, one can always be made from a slide.

Slides seem to present truer color than prints and they are more effective in representing stained glass by treating light through a transparency rather than reflecting it. We like Ektachrome® Daylight color ASA 64; however, color being the very personal choice it is, you might want to experiment with the different films available before settling on one.

## FLASHBULBS

Neither strobes nor flashbulbs are very effective in photographing stained glass because of the "bounce back" of light that invariably occurs. The only way to avoid this is to stand at an extreme angle to the object being photographed. This is not only limiting but probably false to whatever effect the object is meant to produce. It's a little unfair to see something from the side that's meant to be viewed face on.

If sufficient and correct lighting isn't available to take your picture, use a tripod and time exposure. If your camera isn't equipped for this, best to skip the picture altogether. It will only be a waste of film.

## MIRROR

Speaking of face-on pictures, photographing mirror is a good way to get your face on one. Since this is undesirable, you have two ways to go. You can cover the mirrored portions with paper cut to size or you can place a large white sheet of paper or cardboard in front of the mirror and shoot from above it. This way the mirrored portion reflects a neutral wall while still very much emphasizing the fact that it is mirror. A projection screen can be utilized for this. Don't use more screen than necessary to enable you to maneuver the shot from as small an angle as possible, and don't use anything more reflective than white paper. Such material will bounce your light back to the object being considered and cause unwanted glare.

## DEVELOPING YOUR OWN

As we said earlier, you may eventually come to this. Other than being lots of fun, having your own darkroom cuts a lot of costs. It enables you not only to develop your own photos, but to shoot as many as necessary for the most perfect composition, detail or beauty. Also, you can make larger prints than might be economically feasible by commercial labs and you can develop more of them.

There's a particular satisfaction in carrying the process through from designing, cutting and leading the glass to taking the definitive pictures. If things go wrong along the line, you've only yourself to blame. And if praise is due, that too is all yours.

# Glossary

*Beading:* The act of passing solder over a rim of foil to raise the edge and provide a more pleasing look while adding strength to the joint. A comparatively cool soldering iron is necessary. If it becomes too hot, the solder will flatten out rather than rise and bead.

*Dalle-de-verre:* This is also called "chunk glass." Dalles are thick (about 1") slabs of colored glass which are usually broken to shape with a special hammer and anvil, though a masonry hammer and chisel may do. You can acquire pieces of dalle for nothing at some stained glass studios where they may store boxfuls of such addenda to larger projects.

*Double glazed:* Literally "glazed twice." This occurs where two pieces of glass are laid on top of each other and bound together with lead came, foil or even glue. Advantages of this technique are to modify existing hues of glass, one by another, and to present a textured appearance to a flat plane by judicious elevations of certain portions of the foreground. Tiffany made extensive use of this technique in many of his windows wherein faces, hands and sometimes entire figures are double glazed.

*Drapery glass:* An old type of opalescent sheet glass with extensive rippling of the surface making it look like folds of drapery or clothing. Quite hard to cut.

*Etching:* This implies the use of some method to wear away portions of the surface color of a piece of "flashed" (two-tone) glass for an artistic (or merely curious) effect. Hydrofluoric acid is best used but it is dangerous and should only be handled by an expert. We have spoken of alternate methods of etching in the text.

*Farbigem technique:* A method implying a "sandwiching" of colored glass between sheets of plastic to provide a three-dimensional effect in an attempt to achieve depth.

*Flashed glass:* Sheets of glass that have a double color on one surface. When the top color is etched away, the bottom shows through. Such glass has a particular sheen all its own and may be used for its mixture of color hues rather than as etching glass.

*Flints:* These are planned (as opposed to accidental) breaks in a monotonous linear flow such as diamonds or rectangles. An occasional flint of the same or another color may be used as the top or bottom portion of individual geometrics. It's a technique that can't be overused or it will look as though you dropped the window and just patched it back together.

*Foil:* This is copper tape, adhesive backed on one side. This material is used in electronics and in stained glass. In glasswork the copper is wrapped around the glass edges, furnishing a soldering rim for attachment of the individual pieces.

*Fusing:* The act of partially melting selected pieces of glass together or into a background surface, usually glass as well. Pieces of glass may be fused together and then imbedded into plastic as a background. This process can be accomplished with a torch but it is limited to small pieces of glass only. Most fusing must be done in a kiln. Attempting to heat any substantial piece of glass with a point flame, such as a torch, is dangerous. The glass is likely to shatter all over you.

*Gemmaux:* A mosaic-type use of glass rather like textured painting. Pieces of glass may be piled one over another to achieve the desired effect.

*Groze:* The act of gnawing away slivers and pinpoints from glass edges, to doing an actual carving job on certain tortuously designed pieces. For the purpose, a special pliers called a "grozing" pliers must be used. Don't try it with electrician's pliers; chances are you'll break up a lot of glass this way.

*Kiln wash:* The special powder used in the kiln as a bed for the glass that is to be fired. This material is able to take extremely high heat without clumping together. It must stay clean and must not react with or stick to the glass. Kiln wash, more than a kiln shelf, helps distribute a uniform heat over the glass.

*Lamination:* This is a type of double glazing though usually there is something contained within the two layers of glass. It may be a pressed flower, it may be a painted element—it may even be another type of glass. The whole is bonded together, forming one resultant piece.

*Lava:* A nice, soft rock that can be used for bases with glass projects. It can be carved or drilled with ease.

*Lead poisoning:* Though we have never seen a result of lead poisoning from working with stained glass, some people may be careless enough to achieve such an undesirable situation. One case was recently reported in the *New England Journal of Medicine.* Always work in a well ventilated room and clean hands well after work is over. Never eat with hands still dirty from lead oxides. We do not feel that gloves or a mask are at all necessary; we never use such items. Our experience has been that good sanitary habits will prevent any ill effects from the material. Be careful not to inhale any of the fumes from soldering. Allow your workshop enough space so that such fumes do not mount up. Our feeling is that you would have to work pretty hard to get into trouble this way. No one we have ever met has.

*Lightbox:* One way to display a panel without having to worry about outside light is to display it in a lightbox. The end result need be no heavier than a good size picture and can be far more effective.

*Multiple glazing:* Similar to double glazing but implying the use of three or more layers of glass.

*Resist material:* Any spreadable substance that will not be affected by acid used for etching, such as asphaltum. Plastic may also be used. Such material is spread over the surface to be etched and appropriate holes are cut into it where the etching process is desired.

*Rondels:* Machine made circles of glass either pressed or spun. They come in varied sizes and are quite lovely just by themselves.

*Routing:* Cutting a ledge into a piece of wood to enable glass to fit in a recessed manner. This is then usually held in with molding. Routing must be done exactly or the impressed glass will wobble.

*Silk screen:* A process of printing onto different materials including glass. It is a mass production technique rather than a one-of-a-kind result.

*Squeegee:* A sweep to gather ink onto the silk screen and impress it onto the material to be printed when doing the silk screen process. It is usually made of rubber or plastic.

*Stencil:* A cutout of a design to be painted or silk-screened. Special stencil paper or even metal may be used to prepare stencils.

*Stick light:* On a painted surface, that light allowed to penetrate by scraping away portions of the paint. This can be done with a feather or a brush or a stick.

*Tack:* Temporary soldering of two surfaces with small dabs of solder bridging across rather than a complete fixing. This allows for changes in the design or glass color by comparison with surrounding pieces since a tacked piece is much easier to unsolder than one firmly placed.

# Sources
# of Supply

Art Glass of Illinois
105 Oakwood Park
East Peoria, IL 61611

Cline Glass Co., Inc.
1135 SE Grand Ave.
Portland, OR 97214

Endeavor Products, Ltd.
443 East First Ave.
Roselle, NJ 07203

Franklin Glass Art Studio
222 East Sycamore St.
Columbus, OH 43206

Glass Haus Studio
1819 South Alameda
Corpus Christi, TX 78404

Glass House Studio, Inc.
125 State St.
St. Paul, MN 55107

Glass Masters, Inc.
154 West 18th St.
New York, NY 10010

Nervo Distributors
650 University Ave.
Berkeley, CA 94710

New Renaissance Glass Works
5151 Broadway
Oakland, CA 94611

Pendleton Studios
3895 North Tulsa Ave.
Oklahoma City, OK 73112

Northwest Art Glass
904 Elliott Ave. West
Seattle, WA 98117

The Stained Glass Club
P.O. Box 244
Norwood, NJ 07648

Stained Glass Forest
2312 K St.
Sacramento, CA 95816

Ed Hoy's Stained Glass
999 East Chicago Ave.
Naperville, IL 60540

Tiffany Stained Glass Ltd.
549 N. Wells St.
Chicago, IL 60610

The Stained Glass Shoppe
2315 North 45th St.
Seattle, WA 98103

Stained Glass & Supplies, Inc.
2104 Colorado Blvd.
Los Angeles, CA 90041

Tiffany Touch
337 West 21st St.
Norfolk, VA 23517

Yesterday's Glass
110 West Colonial Drive
Orlando, FL 32801

Village Hobby Mart
2414 Bolsover
Houston, TX 77005

Glassart Studio of America, Inc.
510 S. 52nd St., Suite 104
Tempe, AZ 85281

Dianne's Crafts
18021 Chatsworth
Granada Hills, CA 91344

Franciscan Glass Co.
100 San Antonio Rd.
Mountain View, CA 94040

Mad Dog
18615 Topham St.
Reseda, CA 91335

Scarab Glass Works
729 Divisadero
Fresno, CA 93721

The Stained Pane
3160 E. La Palma Ave., Unit M
Anaheim, CA 92806

Stephens Stained Glass Studio
9637 Magnolia Ave.
Riverside, CA 92503

D & L Stained Glass Supply
4919 N. Broadway
Boulder, CO 80302

Rocky Mountain Arts & Crafts
5660 S. Syracuse Cir.
Englewood, CO 80110

Stanford Art Glass
513 Manitou Ave.
Manitou Springs, CO 80829

Stained Glass Gallery
5423 North Federal Highway
Fort Lauderdale, FL 33308

Jennifer's Glassworks
2410 Piedmont Rd., N.E.
Atlanta, GA 30324

Landin's Lamps
2329 13th St.
Moline, IL 61265

The Macrame Man
127 N. Main St.
Decatur, IL 62521

Stained Glass of Barrington
712 S. Northwest Hwy.
Barrington, IL 60010

Delphi Craft Supply Center
2224 E. Michigan
Lansing, MI 48912

Rainbow Resources
1503 Lake Drive, S.E.
Grand Rapids, MI 49506

Houston Stained Glass Supply
1829 Arlington
Houston, TX 77008

Aladdin Stained Glass
1131 East Yandell Drive
El Paso, TX 79902

Occidental Associates
410 Occidental South
Seattle, WA 98104

Arts & Crafts Studio
7120 Little River Turnpike
Annandale, VA 22003

J. Ring Studio Company
2125 East Hennepin
Minneapolis, MN 55413

Classical Glass, Inc.
175 Church St.
Burlington, VT 05401

Buffalo Plate & Window
   Glass Corp.
1245 E. Ferry St.
Buffalo, NY 14211

Saylescraft, Inc.
171 Main St.
Nyack, NY 10960

E. H. Watkeys, Jr.
463 Easton Rd.
Horsham, PA 19004

# Suggested
# Reading

BOOKS

Allcock, Hubert: *Heraldic Design,* Tudor, NY, 1962.
Anderson, Harriette: *Kiln-Fired Glass,* Chilton, Radnor, PA, 1970.
Bernstein, Jack: *Stained Glass Craft,* Macmillan, NY, 1973.
Biegeleisen, J. I.: *The Complete Book of Silk Screen Printing Production,* Dover, NY, 1963.
Birkner, Heinrich: *Screen Printing,* Sterling, NY, 1972.
Franklyn, Julian: *Heraldry,* Barnes, NY, 1965.
French, Jennie: *Glass-Works. The Copper Foil Technique of Stained Glass,* Van Nostrand, NY, 1974.
Gillon, Edmund: *Art Nouveau: An Anthology from the Studio,* Dover, NY, 1969.
Goldsmith-Carter, George: *Sailing Ships and Sailing Craft,* Bantam, NY, 1971.
Gruber, Elmar: *Nail Sculpture,* Sterling, NY, 1968.
Hendrickson, Edwin: *Mosaics, Hobby and Art,* Hill & Wang, NY, 1957.
Isenberg, Anita & Seymour: *How To Work In Stained Glass,* Chilton, Radnor, PA, 1972.
————: *Stained Glass Lamps: Construction and Design,* Chilton, Radnor, PA, 1974.
————: *Start Off In Stained Glass,* Chilton, Radnor, PA, 1974.
Kronquist, Emil: *Metalwork for Craftsmen,* Dover, NY, 1972.
Luciano: *Stained Glass Lamps and Terrariums,* Hidden House Press, Palo Alto, CA, 1973.
Mirow, Gregory: *A Treasury of Design for Artists and Craftsmen,* Dover, NY, 1969.
Paterson, James: *Stained Glass,* Museum Press Ltd., London, 1968.
Rothenberg, Polly: *The Complete Book of Creative Glass Art,* Crown, NY, 1974.
Walters, Thomas: *Art Nouveau Graphics,* St. Martin's Press, London, 1971.
Warren, Geoffrey: *Art Nouveau,* Octopus Books, London, 1972.

MAGAZINES

The following magazines deal either in toto or in part with stained glass as a craft, hobby or aesthetic experience. Almost all of them provide a marketplace for ideas and sales through their advertisements and articles.

*Artisan Crafts.* Star Route #4, Box 179-F, Reeds Spring, MO 65737

*Country Wide Crafts.* Country Wide Publications, Inc., 222 Park Avenue South, New York, NY 10003

*Craft Horizons.* The American Crafts Council, 44 West 53rd Street, New York, NY 10020

*Creative Crafts.* Model Craftsman Publishing Corporation, 31 Arch Street, Ramsey, NJ 07446

*Glass Art Magazine:* P.O. Box 7527, Oakland, CA 94615

*Glass: The Complete Magazine for the Serious Collector.* Special Publications, Inc., 5 Lincoln Court, Princeton, NJ 08540

*Leonardo: International Journal of the Contemporary Artist.* 17 Rue Emile Dunois, 92 Boulogne sur Seine, France

*Popular Ceramics.* Popular Ceramic Publications, Inc., 6011 Santa Monica Boulevard, Los Angeles, CA 90038

*Popular Crafts.* Challenge Publications, Inc., 7950 Deering Avenue, Canoga Park, CA 91304

*Saturday Review of the Arts.* Saturday Review Inc., 450 Pacific Avenue, San Francisco, CA 94101

*Stained Glass: The Magazine of the Stained Glass Association of America.* 66 Malin Road, Malvern, PA 19355

*The Glass Workshop.* The Stained Glass Club, P.O. Box 244, Norwood, NJ 07648

*The Metropolitan Museum of Art: Bulletins.* The Metropolitan Museum of Art, Fifth Avenue and 82nd Street, New York, NY 10028

*Your Church.* The Religious Publishing Co., 198 Allendale Road, King of Prussia, PA 19406

# Index

Anita Isenberg was born in New York City and attended high
school in Tucson, Arizona, and then went on to the University of
Tempe in that state. She did graduate work in art and design abroad
and at that time her interest in stained glass became activated.

She was an apprentice at William O'Connor's Castle Hill Studio
from 1963 to 1966 and then opened her own studio, the Stained Glass
Club. She has executed commissions for windows, lamps and objets
d'art in stained glass for the past twelve years during which time she
also taught the craft in her studio and in colleges, high schools, adult
evening classes and aboard ship—which led to her lecturing in Suva,
Fiji and Casablanca, Morocco, among other exotic places. Under the
name "Anita De" she is also editor of her own journal of stained glass
and allied arts, "The Glass Workshop" which enjoys a large circulation
in this country and abroad. She is currently working on a book consid-
ering all aspects of glass painting and staining.

Seymour Isenberg is a graduate of Horace Mann School in New York
City, Syracuse University and Kansas City College of Osteopathy &
Surgery. He is co-author (with L. M. Elting) of "You Can Be Fat-
Free Forever". His latest book in conjunction with L. M. Elting, "The
Consumer's Guide to Successful Surgery" has just been published by
St. Martin's Press. He is currently working on a hospital mystery titled
"Emergency Exit." He is a contributor to medical, crafts and wildlife
journals. The Isenbergs live in New Jersey.

# About
# the Authors